ROUTLEDGE · ENGLISH TEXTS

GENERAL ED

ALFRED, LORD TENNYSON

Selected Poetry

ROUTLEDGE · ENGLISH · TEXTS
GENERAL EDITOR · JOHN DRAKAKIS

ALFRED, LORD TENNYSON

Selected Poetry

Edited by Norman Page

LONDON AND NEW YORK

First published 1995
by Routledge
11 New Fetter Lane,
London EC4P 4EE

Simultaneously published in the
USA and Canada
by Routledge
29 West 35th Street, New York,
NY 10001

Introduction, editorial material
©1995 Norman Page

Typeset in Bembo 9 on 11½ by
Florencetype Ltd, Stoodleigh, Devon

Printed and bound in Great Britain by
Clays Ltd, St Ives plc

British Library Cataloguing in
Publication Data
A catalogue record for this book is available
from the British Library

Library of Congress Cataloguing in
Publication Data
A catalogue record for this book has been
requested

ISBN 0–415–07724–9

Contents

Note on the text

The text followed in this selection is that of the Eversley edition, prepared by Tennyson's son Hallam and published in nine volumes in 1907–8, which embodies the poet's final intentions. Tennyson was an inveterate reviser of his own work, sometimes returning to a poem and making changes after an interval of half a century or more, and the history of his published texts is a complex one. At the same time many of his revisions are of great interest, and attention is drawn to a few of the more striking instances in the notes to this selection (see, for example, under 'The Lady of Shalott'). For more comprehensive information, Christopher Ricks's edition should be consulted.

Introduction

Tennyson had both a longer life than the average for his time and an exceptionally long creative life. Writing his earliest poems in childhood, he continued into old age, so that his career is comparable in this respect with that of, among others, Hardy and Yeats. Like them, he survived into an age radically different from that in which he had grown up, and his work expresses some of the problems and tensions involved in coming to terms with change. He was born in the year in which Byron set out on the Grand Tour, lived through six-sevenths of the entire Victorian age, and died in the year of Oscar Wilde's fateful meeting with Lord Alfred Douglas. His first volume of poems had been published in the pre-Victorian period, before the passing of the 1832 Reform Bill, and during the lifetime of Wordsworth, Coleridge and Scott; his last appeared in the same year as publications by Henry James, Rudyard Kipling, George Gissing and W. B. Yeats. He practised, moreover, a great diversity of poetic forms, ranging from the brief lyric to the epic.

Different generations of readers and critics have arrived at widely different valuations of the various facets of Tennyson's achievement – valuations that sometimes tell us less about Tennyson than about the values and inhibitions of their own age. Whereas, for instance, his contemporaries esteemed the didacticism and medievalism of his longer poems, later responses have often preferred the shorter, more intense and subjective poems, the 'psychodrama' of the once unfashionable *Maud*, or the occasional poems that commemorate particular friendships.

There are, then, problems of sheer quantity and diversity as well as of relative evaluation in confronting Tennyson's work, and a selection

1

such as this one can never be fully representative but must emphasize certain aspects at the expense of others. For obvious reasons the long narrative poems – the equivalent of short stories or even novels in verse – have been largely (though not entirely) excluded. His Arthurian epic, *Idylls of the King*, which occupied Tennyson for some forty years from start to finish and fills nearly 300 pages in Ricks's edition, has been almost entirely omitted, since brief extracts or even a handful of the dozen long poems that comprise it could give no fair impression of its scale or significance. (An exception has been made in favour of the earliest of the *Idylls*, composed before the scheme was planned and in circumstances of special interest.)

What a selection can do, beyond its basic task of being as fully representative as space permits, is to draw attention to certain aspects of the writer's work that have suffered relative neglect or undervaluation, and this must be the justification for what might otherwise seem some eccentric inclusions – for example, the narrative poem *Enoch Arden* and a number of the very personal poems of Tennyson's later years. Such decisions draw attention to one of the problems facing the reader of a poet who has been so famous for so long and whose work has suffered from overfamiliarity. His poems have been painted, set to music, adapted for the cinema, recited by practitioners of 'elocution', and endlessly quoted (or misquoted) by many who have no idea that the words they are using are Tennyson's, scraps of whose work fill twenty-four closely printed columns in the *Oxford Dictionary of Quotations*. An act of defamiliarization is called for if we are to be fair to Tennyson and to ourselves, and this will also involve overcoming, as far as is possible, the inability of our own age to deal with certain values and sensibilities that the Victorians held dear but which now too readily invoke a sceptical or uncomprehending response – for instance, an idealized form of male friendship or an admiration for self-denial and renunciation. For, like any writer, and in many respects more than is usual, Tennyson was the product of his age as well as its spokesman.

Tennyson was born on 6 August 1809, in the village of Somersby in Lincolnshire where his father was rector. He was the third of his parents' eleven surviving children, and eventually the small rectory must have been crowded to bursting-point – the more so, since many of them, including Alfred, had very little in the way of formal schooling. With a large garden, however, and with fields and a stream nearby, it was an attractive spot in which to grow up, and Tennyson's love of and very close observation of nature dated from this time. It was quite literally close, for he was severely myopic (later portraits show him holding a book very close to his eyes); provided he could get close enough to a tree or a flower, however, he could describe it with unforgettable precision and vividness.

The Reverend George Tennyson was a scholar and a poet, and under his tutoring his son laid the foundations of a sound knowledge of Latin and Greek and also began to write poetry himself. Less happily, the father suffered from mental instability – a hereditary trait to which deep bitterness and resentment (he had in effect been disinherited by his own wealthy father) no doubt contributed – and was subject to fits of black depression that later led to violence. Most of his children, to a greater or lesser extent, suffered some form of mental illness at one time or another, and Tennyson himself, especially in his earlier years, was not immune from long periods of depression and lethargy.

Apart from a few unhappy years at Louth Grammar School, Tennyson remained at home until it was time to go to Trinity College, Cambridge, where he does not seem to have been an outstanding scholar but quickly made his mark as a poet. It is very striking how his contemporaries saw him as a poet of extraordinary promise and found nothing inappropriate in comparing him to Byron and Milton. He was in fact already a published poet since he had, with his brother Charles, published *Poems by Two Brothers* in 1827, when he was only seventeen.

At Cambridge Tennyson formed a number of friendships that were to be lifelong, but the most important and intense of them was also possibly the briefest. Arthur Hallam was an Etonian and the son of a famous historian; his family was not short of money and had homes in London and Somerset. Different though their circumstances were, they became friends, Hallam visited Somersby, and fell in love with one of Tennyson's sisters, to whom he subsequently became engaged. But on a visit to the Continent with his father, Hallam died suddenly and quite unexpectedly of a brain haemorrhage at the age of twenty-two. This was on 15 September 1833, and when the news – travelling slowly from Vienna to rural Lincolnshire – reached Tennyson, he was devastated. The creative effect of his loss, however, was to release a flood of poems and fragments, some of them direct expressions of grief and loss but others conveying much more obliquely the writer's emotional state. 'Ulysses', for instance, is a dramatic monologue drawing on the story of the Greek hero. It was at this time, too, that Tennyson began what was to become, seventeen years later, *In Memoriam*, a long (and long-delayed) tribute to Hallam's memory but also a public poem articulating the anxieties of the age.

Earlier, Tennyson had published two volumes of poems: the first, while he was still an undergraduate, in 1830 (*Poems, Chiefly Lyrical*), the other in 1832 (*Poems*), after he had left Cambridge without taking a degree, shortly after the death of his father. Both had attracted some adverse criticism, and the second had been attacked with particular severity by the veteran reviewer J. W. Croker, who had earlier attacked Keats. His heavily sarcastic ridicule of what he perceived as Tennyson's poetic affectations appeared in the Tory *Quarterly Review* and was to some extent politically motivated, since Croker believed that the young poet was continuing the liberal tradition of the Romantic poets of a dozen years earlier. (Since Keats, Shelley and Byron were all dead by this time, Tennyson was an obvious candidate for consideration as their natural successor.) The result of these attacks was to produce in Tennyson a profound and prolonged sense of self-doubt, and for nearly ten years he published very little – an extraordinary hiatus in the career of a poet who was only just getting into his stride. But as we have seen, the death of Hallam had a powerfully creative effect on his friend and it was during the so-called 'ten years' silence' that the foundations of some of Tennyson's later work were laid.

That silence was broken in 1842 with the publication in two volumes of a collection that included both new material and revised versions of some of the earlier poems. This was one of Tennyson's most important collections and contains some of his best-known poems. Comparison of the original and revised versions of, say, 'The Lady of Shalott' (see the notes in this edition) suggests that the effect of the revisions was to strengthen some of them considerably. Despite the decade's silence so far as publication was concerned, Tennyson was still in his early thirties, but some of the reviews of the 1842 volumes make it clear that he was now becoming recognized as the leading poet of the new generation. Of the Romantic poets only Wordsworth, now in his seventies, survived: the stage was clear for a new chief actor, and Tennyson seemed to have the qualifications for the role. At the same time concern was expressed that his poetry had an element of the self-indulgent, and pressure was being brought to bear upon him to become more didactic and responsible, and to use his art to debate the issues of the day and to give guidance on its problems. It was to be another five years, however, before Tennyson responded with a thoroughly contemporary poem, *The Princess*, which deals with the education and emancipation of women.

During the 1840s Tennyson's friends had been concerned, not without good reason, about his state of mind as well as his physical health. At a stage of life when many writers are at their most productive (his contemporary Dickens is an outstanding example), Tennyson seemed inactive and uncertain of the direction he should follow, as well as being reluctant to publish what he had written (the 1842 collection had appeared only because his friend Edward FitzGerald had carried him off to meet a publisher). His anxieties about his physical health may have been largely hypochondria, but his mental anxieties were real enough and the fear of an inherited tendency to insanity troubled him deeply. It may have been for this reason that his marriage to Emily Sellwood, with whom he had fallen in love in the 1830s, was so long deferred. At the same time his economic prospects were far from brilliant: a legacy had vanished in an unwise speculation, and he had never had any other form of employment than being a poet – never, indeed, seems to have considered such a possibility.

All this changed in 1850, the year that saw his marriage, his appointment to the laureateship, and the publication of *In Memoriam*, the tribute to Hallam on which he had been working intermittently for nearly seventeen years. Marriage brought him stability and peace of mind, and for the first time he had a home of his own; soon afterwards, with the birth of two sons, and the move to Farringford on the Isle of Wight, the moody reclusive young man had been transformed into a paterfamilias and homeowner. It has sometimes been argued that domestication affected Tennyson's poetry for the worse, turning the rebel into a pillar of the establishment and making his later work conventional and conformist, a reflection and celebration of the values of the age rather than a criticism of them. This may, however, be a rather superficial view of such later poems as *Maud* and *Enoch Arden*, and while there are certainly shifts of emphasis in the later work these may be partly explained by the natural wish

5

of a writer, as he grows older, not simply to repeat himself but to set himself new problems and to explore new styles and forms.

Tennyson became Poet Laureate after the death of Wordsworth – an appropriate succession, since he had continued the Romantic tradition, though his earlier work is much closer to Keats than to Wordsworth. Eventually he was to become on friendly terms with Queen Victoria, for whom, after the death of the Prince Consort in 1861, *In Memoriam* was favourite reading. Again, it can be argued that the laureateship had a repressive and conventionalizing effect on Tennyson's work, though it is worth noting that in accepting the appointment – which he did only after some hesitation – he stipulated that there were to be 'no birthday odes' expected of him: in other words, no poems written to order for such occasions as royal birthdays or weddings. He did not quite keep to this resolution, and some of the best-known poems of his later years, such as the 'Ode on the Death of the Duke of Wellington' and 'The Charge of the Light Brigade', fall into the category of public poetry written to commemorate a topical event. At the same time the Laureate remained an essentially private man: enormously popular in his later years, he shunned publicity and for the most part lived very quietly, a celebrity in spite of himself and at times even to his own disgust and irritation.

Though *In Memoriam* was published anonymously, its authorship quickly became known and it became one of the most popular – perhaps, indeed, *the* most popular – long poem of the Victorian age. During its long gestation the private origins, without being lost sight of, had been subsumed under a more generalized concern with issues of faith and doubt. Thousands of thinking readers were to find in it the articulation of their own spiritual anxieties: for example, in reconciling the discoveries of the new science with traditional beliefs based on a literalist interpretation of scripture as the inspired word of God. That it moves, in its conclusion, to a reaffirmation of faith did no harm to its popularity. It was not a conclusion to which all Victorian writers felt able to move: George Eliot and Hardy, for example, experienced the shocks to their early faith but were unable to recover the spiritual equilibrium that had been disturbed. But it is only fair to Tennyson to add that there was nothing complacent or unreflecting about his religious views, and to the end of his life he was still earnestly, even desperately, in search of reassurance on the crucial matter of personal immortality. Though not conventionally religious – he was not, for instance, a regular churchgoer – he was in a true sense a deeply religious man for whom spiritual problems were central to life.

It is worth remembering, too, that even after 1850 he remained for many a controversial figure whose experiments could disturb and even disgust. *Maud* (1854) is an experimental 'monodrama' in which the speaker is a young man racked by emotional distresses that bear a strong resemblance to those that tormented the young Tennyson; he suffers a period of insanity, then recovers and ends by volunteering for service in the Crimean War. From the opening lines the verse has a remarkable tension that looks forward to later dramatic monologues conveying neurosis such as Eliot's 'The Love Song of J. Alfred Prufrock'. Perhaps because it is in some ways a very modern poem it was bitterly attacked by many contemporary critics.

Maud became Tennyson's favourite poem for recitation to friends and visitors; unlike Dickens, he never read his work in public, but he was addicted to, even obsessed by, giving his own renderings of his work to any willing or unresisting audience, even if it consisted of only one person. The point is of some importance since he clearly thought of poetry as a performance art and of a text as something to be spoken and heard. Evidence suggests that his own style of reading or reciting was highly rhetorical and declamatory, almost a chanting rather than a speaking voice, and his concern with metrics and verbal sound-effects needs to be considered in the light of this fact. Near the end of his life he made a wax-cylinder recording of 'The Charge of the Light Brigade', and despite its technical imperfections – and although he was then in his eighties – the recording still gives an idea of his powerful voice, his strong regional accent, and his instinct for a strongly dramatic reading, deliberate and emphatic.

The popularity of Tennyson's poetry, and his personal fame, during the second half of his long lifetime are difficult to grasp in an age that has marginalized poetry but draw attention to a radical difference between mid-Victorian middle-class culture and our own. To cite only one or two examples: when an illustrated edition of his poems was published in 1857, the print-run was 10,000 copies, while seven years later *Enoch Arden and Other Poems* sold 17,000 on the day of publication. He became rich (in the second half of 1864 his income from poetry was well over £6,000, an immense sum at that time), built a second country house, sent his sons to leading public schools, and generally lived in a style appropriate to a country gentleman. It was a Victorian success story and a remarkable case of upward mobility for the parson's son from the crowded rectory in an obscure corner of Lincolnshire. Yet Tennyson's devotion to his art was unwavering, and he remained a poet to the end of his life. Eccentric in dress and sometimes unconventional in his manners and speech, he also looked and behaved like a poet, or like the traditional Romantic conception of a poet: tall, handsome, long-haired, in a cloak and sombrero-type hat that dated back to his visit to Spain as a young man with Arthur Hallam and were retained amid changing fashions to the end of his days. There was probably a sense in which, consciously or otherwise, he cultivated the persona of a poet, insisting on the poet's bardic or vatic role and on his essential difference from other men. While some poets could compromise with the world of affairs – Matthew Arnold, for instance, had become a busy Inspector of Schools – Tennyson never budged an inch in the assertion of his poetic identity.

All of this makes him seem, by modern standards, a picturesque but rather remote figure, and some of the literary enterprises of his later years may now seem difficult to sympathize with and may fail to commend themselves to modern tastes. For some fifteen years from the late 1850s onwards, he was much occupied with the long poem that became *Idylls of the King*, a kind of historical novel, or set of linked short stories, in verse that runs to over 10,000 lines of blank verse. The stories of the legendary King Arthur (a potent name for Tennyson) were much less familiar in the early nineteenth century than they later became, but already in the 1830s Tennyson was evincing a strong interest in medievalism in general, and the Arthurian legends in particular, and had grasped their possibilities for the picturesque and the heroic. 'The Lady of Shalott' and 'Morte d'Arthur' were early and important results of this interest.

After the death of the Prince Consort, the legendary Arthur, already coloured by the embalmed memory of Arthur Hallam, also absorbed elements from the dead Albert: a literary source was given greater potency through modern associations and analogues, both private and public. Further poems were written and published, the last not appearing until 1885. The *Idylls* were widely popular in their own day; that they are now unfashionable is no doubt partly due to the high-minded ethos they embody and the story-book quality of their medievalism (Gerard Manley Hopkins described them as 'Charades from the Middle Ages'), but also reflects our own inability to cope with narrative verse.

With the *Idylls* virtually complete by the mid-1870s, Tennyson turned to another medium, the theatre. His plays are little read and even less performed today, though they were produced in their day, in some cases very successfully. Behind them is the impulse to emulate, or at least pay homage to, Shakespeare: most of the Romantic poets had written verse-dramas, many of the Victorian poets also did so, and Tennyson was no exception. Like the *Idylls*, they tend to take on historical subjects. Their length and necessary impersonality make them the opposite of those parts of Tennyson's work in which are to be found the qualities nowadays most valued: the intense, poignant, often brief expression of personal feeling. But this may be merely another way of saying that each generation values those parts of Tennyson's work (as it does with other writers) that endorse its own prejudices and harmonize with its sensibilities, and undervalues those parts that fail to do so.

There is, in any case, quite another side of Tennyson to be found in the short poems written during the same period. Particularly fine is a number of poems written to, or to the memory of, particular friends or relations such as Edward FitzGerald, Rosa Baring, W. H. Brookfield, Mary Boyle, Sir John Simeon – and, inevitably, the two most important persons in Tennyson's emotional life, Arthur Hallam and his own wife Emily. These are, in origin at least, private poems, and their tone, in contrast to the rhetoric and conscious manipulations of the public poetry, is quiet and restrained, and sometimes even humorous. (Except in a handful of poems in the Lincolnshire dialect, there is not a lot of humour in Tennyson's poetry, though he seems to have been a man who loved a joke, bawdy if possible: his concept of the poet's role, and of poetry as the highest form of literary art, compelled a seriousness that excluded from it the expression of certain areas of his personality.) For one who had been moody, reclusive and difficult in his early years, Tennyson had a surprising capacity for friendship, and in his later years his large circle of friends came from many walks of life: not just fellow-authors but artists, musicians, politicians, theologians and churchmen, headmasters and dons, landowners and aristocrats, and

9

others. Especially in the poems, like 'The Roses on the Terrace', that bring together the present and the distant past, there is a wonderfully subtle use of language, image and verse to convey the workings of the remembering mind, and it has seemed worth grouping these poems together in the present selection even though doing so involves some departure from strict chronology.

As some of the above comments have suggested, there is a perceptible contrast, more marked in the second half of Tennyson's lifetime, between his 'private' and his 'public' poems, though there are also instances which blur the distinction. While his contemporaries tended to prefer the poems that spoke out on public issues or dealt with events in the public domain (*In Memoriam*, the 'Wellington' ode, 'The Charge of the Light Brigade', etc.), modern tastes are likely to favour the shorter, more subjective and more concentrated poems, both those in which feeling is directly expressed and those in which it is mediated through a persona, as in 'Ulysses' and 'Mariana'. Tennyson's art embraces both kinds, and this selection has attempted to represent both as fully as possible.

Like anyone who lives longer than average, Tennyson found his last years saddened by the death of many relations and friends, and some of the poems addressed to individuals that have been referred to are poems of mourning and commemoration. A particular grief was the death in his early thirties of his second son, Lionel, from a tropical disease contracted during a visit to India. (See 'To the Marquis of Dufferin and Ava'.) His other son, Hallam, left Cambridge (as his father had done) without a degree after his mother suffered a breakdown through overwork. Emily had taken upon herself the huge task of protecting Tennyson from an eager and intrusive public who wanted to besiege him with letters, books and visits; Emily saw her role as preserving the conditions in which he could lead his creative life, and became an unpaid and grossly overworked secretary, dealing (among other things) with a huge correspondence, until her health gave way. Hallam instantly took her place and remained faithful until his father's death – indeed, long after that, for he also became Tennyson's first biographer, his pious *Memoir* of 1897 being still an essential source for Tennysonian biography. Hallam inherited the peerage that had been bestowed on Tennyson in 1883 – the first poet to be honoured in this way – and the title is still extant.

Tennyson died on 6 October 1892. He had remained active until very near the end, and had given the last of many readings of *Maud* only six weeks earlier. His funeral in Westminster Abbey was thronged and his death and burial were extensively covered in the press, some reports referring to him as the most famous Englishman of the age. It seems at first a startling judgement, but it is not easy to think of rivals – which brings us back, once again, to the centrality of poetry in the literary culture and indeed the general cultural life of the time. Tennyson's career would hardly have been possible either earlier or later, and his involvement with his period was an intimate one on many levels.

Like most writers now firmly placed within the established canon, Tennyson has been subject to some fairly dramatic fluctuations of fame. Although, as we have seen, his friends recognized his genius very early, the critics (most of them men of an older and more conservative generation) were more grudging with their praise and sometimes actively hostile. Some of the most favourable early reviews are in fact by friends anxious to help launch his literary career; thus Hallam produced a very interesting review of the 1830 volume and another Cambridge friend, James Spedding, later reviewed the 1842 collection. (Substantial extracts from these and most of the other items cited in this section are conveniently given in John Jump's *Tennyson: The Critical Heritage*.) While the 1830 *Poems, Chiefly Lyrical* was on the whole kindly received, the 1832 *Poems* met with a cooler reception; mention has already been made of the virulent review by J. W. Croker and its long-term effect upon Tennyson's morale and publishing record. His sensitivity to criticism was always intense, and later in life he was reported as saying that 'all the praise he had ever received didn't outweigh for the moment a spiteful and unkindly criticism, even though the criticism ... was directed against the straightness of his toe-nail'. Croker's crudely sarcastic attack – he refers, for instance, to 'the peculiar brilliancy of some of the gems that irradiate [Tennyson's] poetical crown' before pouring ridicule on particular poems and lines – was, in part at least, a political response to favourable reviews in liberal and radical periodicals. In view of Tennyson's later image as a pillar of the establishment it is worth remembering that as a young man he was identified with what would now be called left-wing sympathies.

Almost ten years later the 1842 collection was much more warmly received. Tennyson was now hailed as a poet of great promise, though the point was repeatedly made that he needed to tackle more serious contemporary themes and to concern himself with humanity and moral teaching – in other words, to turn his back on Romantic subjectivism in favour of social responsibility and didacticism. Although no longer very young, he was still seen as a dilettante who had not yet settled down to the proper duties of his calling. He was also urged to write a long poem, the traditional test of poetic commitment. The rest of Tennyson's career showed a willingness to go some of the way, though not all the way, towards meeting these demands. *The Princess* (1847), a long poem on a topical subject, was praised by some though not all reviewers. R. H. Horne, for example, believed that Tennyson had still not realized his full potential: 'He constantly gives us the impression of something greater than his works'. By the end of this decade, when Tennyson had passed his fortieth birthday, he was widely admired but the view was still held that something was missing from his work.

In Memoriam (1850) went a long way towards satisfying the demand for a long poem that seriously addressed important issues and showed a concern for humanity and its predicament at a particular historical moment. It was also probably, crucial in securing its author the laureateship. The picturesqueness and apparent escapism of the early poems on mythological subjects had been left behind; what had taken their place was a readily intelligible exploration, both grave and tender, of the universal human themes of love and death, faith and doubt: themes to which many a Victorian bosom could return an echo. Charles Kingsley's effusive praise was no doubt paralleled by many more informal and unrecorded responses to this poem: 'Blessed, thrice blessed, to find that hero-worship is not yet passed away; that the heart of man still beats young and fresh'. This was not the kind of reaction that the earlier poems had elicited, and its effect was to turn *In Memoriam* into a kind of modern appendage to the Bible. The sales of the poem were very good, with five editions being called for within a year and a half of first publication, and it remained a favourite for the rest of Tennyson's life and beyond.

Maud (1854), on the other hand, was bitterly attacked. Its experimental structure and style were judged obscure, while its portrayal of obsession and neurosis was castigated as unhealthy. Walter Bagehot wrote that 'The subject was calculated to call out the unhealthier sort of youthful imaginations.' It became possible, however, to dismiss *Maud* as a temporary aberration, for five years later the first four of what were to become *Idylls of the King* struck many readers as a welcome return to the responsible didacticism of *In Memoriam*, combined now with a picturesque medieval setting. A long review by W. E. Gladstone, who was to become prime minister a few years later, considered the eligibility of the Arthurian stories for epic treatment, and concluded that 'while we presume nothing, we do not despair of seeing Mr Tennyson achieve on the basis he has chosen the structure of a full-formed epic'. In many respects, therefore, Tennyson was during the 1850s, the central period of his life, fulfilling the demands made on him by his early critics.

As already indicated, Tennyson enjoyed astonishing fame and material success in the second half of his life, and criticism of his work became more uniformly respectful. A common reservation, however, was expressed with regard to the high polish and excessive ornateness of his style and technique: what Matthew Arnold called 'an extreme subtlety and curious elaborateness of expression'. Responding to the *Enoch Arden* volume of 1864 in a letter written on 10 September of that year, Gerard Manley Hopkins, who was then an Oxford undergraduate, described the Tennysonian style as 'Parnassian', adding that, whereas in the finest kind of poetry 'every beauty takes you as it were by surprise', 'in Parnassian pieces you feel that if you were the poet you could have gone on as he has done, you see yourself doing it'. The shock-tactics of Hopkins's own poetry were of course to imply a firm rejection of the Parnassian and the Tennysonian model. Nor was Hopkins alone in his relegation of Tennyson's work to an inferior rank: Bagehot's 1864 essay on 'Pure, Ornate, and Grotesque Art in English Poetry' used Tennyson as an example of 'ornate' art, in which the highly developed treatment is disproportionate to the material. (His examples of 'pure' and 'grotesque' art were, respectively, Wordsworth and Browning.) The complaint that Tennyson is 'literary' and derivative was to prove a persistent one.

Such charges were, however, a minority view during Tennyson's lifetime, and his popularity during his later years, in America as well as England, was not seriously challenged. The reaction after his death was inevitable and was shared by other great Victorian writers who had had a wide and reverential following in their time (for instance, Dickens and George Eliot). In relation to the very different principles and practices of the Modernists, Tennyson's poetry seemed old-fashioned and irrelevant to a rapidly changing world and his diction seemed lacking in vitality and variety, while the international character of literary modernism led his work to be judged parochial.

A landmark in the rehabilitation of Tennyson was Harold Nicolson's study of 1923. A little later, while advocates of 'practical criticism' such as F. R. Leavis had disparaged Tennyson's work as lacking in the requisite qualities of irony and ambiguity, a seminal essay on 'Tears, idle tears' in 1949 by the American critic Cleanth Brooks argued that it is possible to discern these qualities even in Tennyson. The lead was thus given for a new view of Tennyson as not merely the outmoded Victorian patriarch of letters but a complex and subtle poet who had much to offer modern readers.

In the past generation or two, Tennyson has been subjected to and well served by the full range of modern critical and scholarly approaches. As well as important general studies by Jerome Hamilton Buckley, Elaine Jordan, Valerie Pitt, Christopher Ricks, Paul Turner and others, there have been many more specialized approaches to his work and its context. W. D. Paden, for example, has explored the sources and imagery of the early poems; F. E. L. Priestley, David Shaw and Alan Sinfield have all written well on his language and style; Marion Shaw has examined his sexual politics; and Ann C. Colley has discussed the role of madness in his life and work. Marion Shaw's useful bibliography also demonstrates that some individual poems have been extensively discussed – not only *In Memoriam* and *Maud* but, perhaps slightly less predictably, *Idylls of the King*, 47 items relating to which are listed, a high proportion of them published in the last two decades. The fine biography by Robert Bernard Martin and the definitive edition of the poems by Christopher Ricks have also provided the serious student of Tennyson with the indispensable scholarly tools.

ALFRED, LORD TENNYSON

Selected Poetry

MARIANA

'Mariana in the moated grange.'
Measure for Measure

With blackest moss the flower-plots
   Were thickly crusted, one and all:
The rusted nails fell from the knots
   That held the pear to the gable-wall.
The broken sheds look'd sad and strange:
   Unlifted was the clinking latch;
   Weeded and worn the ancient thatch
Upon the lonely moated grange.
      She only said, 'My life is dreary,
         He cometh not,' she said;
      She said, 'I am aweary, aweary,
         I would that I were dead!'   10

Her tears fell with the dews at even;
   Her tears fell ere the dews were dried;
She could not look on the sweet heaven,
   Either at morn or eventide.
After the flitting of the bats,
   When thickest dark did trance the sky,
   She drew her casement-curtain by,
And glanced athwart the glooming flats.
      She only said, 'The night is dreary,
         He cometh not,' she said;
      She said, 'I am aweary, aweary,
         I would that I were dead!'   20

Upon the middle of the night,
   Waking she heard the night-fowl crow:
The cock sung out an hour ere light:
   From the dark fen the oxen's low
Came to her: without hope of change,
   In sleep she seem'd to walk forlorn,
   Till cold winds woke the gray-eyed morn   30

* Numbers in square brackets refer to pages on which notes may be found.

About the lonely moated grange.
  She only said, 'The day is dreary,
   He cometh not,' she said;
  She said, 'I am aweary, aweary,
   I would that I were dead!'

About a stone-cast from the wall
 A sluice with blacken'd waters slept,
And o'er it many, round and small,
 The cluster'd marish-mosses crept.   40
Hard by a poplar shook alway,
 All silver-green with gnarled bark:
 For leagues no other tree did mark
The level waste, the rounding gray.
  She only said, 'My life is dreary,
   He cometh not,' she said;
  She said, 'I am aweary, aweary,
   I would that I were dead!'

And ever when the moon was low,
 And the shrill winds were up and away,   50
In the white curtain, to and fro,
 She saw the gusty shadow sway.
But when the moon was very low,
 And wild winds bound within their cell,
 The shadow of the poplar fell
Upon her bed, across her brow.
  She only said, 'The night is dreary,
   He cometh not,' she said;
  She said, 'I am aweary, aweary,
   I would that I were dead!'   60

All day within the dreamy house,
 The doors upon their hinges creak'd;
The blue fly sung in the pane; the mouse
 Behind the mouldering wainscot shriek'd,
Or from the crevice peer'd about.
 Old faces glimmer'd thro' the doors,
 Old footsteps trod the upper floors,

Old voices called her from without.
 She only said, 'My life is dreary,
  He cometh not,' she said;
 She said, 'I am aweary, aweary,
  I would that I were dead!'

The sparrow's chirrup on the roof,
 The slow clock ticking, and the sound
Which to the wooing wind aloof
 The poplar made, did all confound
Her sense; but most she loathed the hour
 When the thick-moted sunbeam lay
 Athwart the chambers, and the day
Was sloping toward his western bower.
 Then, said she, 'I am very dreary,
  He will not come,' she said;
 She wept, 'I am aweary, aweary,
  Oh God, that I were dead!'

SONG

I

A spirit haunts the year's last hours
Dwelling amid these yellowing bowers:
 To himself he talks;
For at eventide, listening earnestly,
At his work you may hear him sob and sigh
 In the walks;
 Earthward he boweth the heavy stalks
Of the mouldering flowers:
 Heavily hangs the broad sunflower
  Over its grave i' the earth so chilly;
 Heavily hangs the hollyhock,
  Heavily hangs the tiger-lily.

II

The air is damp, and hush'd, and close,
As a sick man's room when he taketh repose
 An hour before death;

19

My very heart faints and my whole soul grieves
At the moist rich smell of the rotting leaves,
    And the breath
    Of the fading edges of box beneath,
And the year's last rose.   20
    Heavily hangs the broad sunflower
      Over its grave i' the earth so chilly;
    Heavily hangs the hollyhock,
      Heavily hangs the tiger-lily.

THE LADY OF SHALOTT

Part I

On either side the river lie
Long fields of barley and of rye,
That clothe the wold and meet the sky;
And thro' the field the road runs by
    To many-tower'd Camelot;
And up and down the people go,
Gazing where the lilies blow
Round an island there below,
    The island of Shalott.

Willows whiten, aspens quiver,   10
Little breezes dusk and shiver
Thro' the wave that runs for ever
By the island in the river
  Flowing down to Camelot.
Four gray walls, and four gray towers,
Overlook a space of flowers,
And the silent isle imbowers
    The Lady of Shalott.

By the margin, willow-veil'd,
Slide the heavy barges trail'd   20
By slow horses; and unhail'd
The shallop flitteth silken-sail'd
    Skimming down to Camelot:

But who hath seen her wave her hand?
Or at the casement seen her stand?
Or is she known in all the land,
    The Lady of Shalott?

Only reapers, reaping early
In among the bearded barley,
Hear a song that echoes cheerly   30
From the river winding clearly,
    Down to tower'd Camelot:
And by the moon the reaper weary,
Piling sheaves in uplands airy,
Listening, whispers ''Tis the fairy
    Lady of Shalott.'

Part II

There she weaves by night and day
A magic web with colours gay.
She has heard a whisper say,
A curse is on her if she stay   40
    To look down to Camelot.
She knows not what the curse may be,
And so she weaveth steadily,
And little other care hath she,
    The Lady of Shalott.

And moving thro' a mirror clear
That hangs before her all the year,
Shadows of the world appear.
There she sees the highway near
    Winding down to Camelot: 50
There the river eddy whirls,
And there the surly village-churls,
And the red cloaks of market girls,
    Pass onward from Shalott.

Sometimes a troop of damsels glad,
An abbot on an ambling pad,
Sometimes a curly shepherd-lad,

Or long-hair'd page in crimson clad,
    Goes by to tower'd Camelot;
And sometimes thro' the mirror blue   60
The knights come riding two and two:
She hath no loyal knight and true,
    The Lady of Shalott.

But in her web she still delights
To weave the mirror's magic sights,
For often thro' the silent nights
A funeral, with plumes and lights
    And music, went to Camelot:
Or when the moon was overhead,
Came two young lovers lately wed;   70
'I am half sick of shadows,' said
    The Lady of Shalott.

Part III

A bow-shot from her bower-eaves,
He rode between the barley-sheaves,
The sun came dazzling thro' the leaves,
And flamed upon the brazen greaves
    Of bold Sir Lancelot.
A red-cross knight for ever kneel'd
To a lady in his shield,
That sparkled on the yellow field,   80
    Beside remote Shalott.

The gemmy bridle glitter'd free,
Like to some branch of stars we see
Hung in the golden Galaxy.
The bridle bells rang merrily
    As he rode down to Camelot:
And from his blazon'd baldric slung
A mighty silver bugle hung,
And as he rode his armour rung,
    Beside remote Shalott.   90

All in the blue unclouded weather
Thick-jewell'd shone the saddle-leather,
The helmet and the helmet-feather
Burn'd like one burning flame together,
    As he rode down to Camelot.
As often thro' the purple night,
Below the starry clusters bright,
Some bearded meteor, trailing light,
    Moves over still Shalott.

His broad clear brow in sunlight glow'd;   100
On burnish'd hooves his war-horse trode;
From underneath his helmet flow'd
His coal-black curls as on he rode,
    As he rode down to Camelot.
From the bank and from the river
He flash'd into the crystal mirror,
'Tirra lirra,' by the river
    Sang Sir Lancelot.

She left the web, she left the loom,
She made three paces thro' the room,
She saw the water-lily bloom,
She saw the helmet and the plume,
    She look'd down to Camelot.
Out flew the web and floated wide;
The mirror crack'd from side to side;
'The curse is come upon me,' cried
    The Lady of Shalott.

Part IV

In the stormy east-wind straining,
The pale yellow woods were waning,
The broad stream in his banks complaining,   120
Heavily the low sky raining
    Over tower'd Camelot;
Down she came and found a boat
Beneath a willow left afloat,
And round about the prow she wrote
    The Lady of Shalott.

And down the river's dim expanse
Like some bold seër in a trance,
Seeing all his own mischance –
With a glassy countenance
    Did she look to Camelot.
And at the closing of the day
She loosed the chain, and down she lay;
The broad stream bore her far away,
    The Lady of Shalott.

Lying, robed in snowy white
That loosely flew to left and right –
The leaves upon her falling light –
Thro' the noises of the night
    She floated down to Camelot:
And as the boat-head wound along
The willowy hills and fields among,
They heard her singing her last song,
    The Lady of Shalott.

Heard a carol, mournful, holy,
Chanted loudly, chanted lowly,
Till her blood was frozen slowly,
And her eyes were darken'd wholly,
    Turn'd to tower'd Camelot.
For ere she reach'd upon the tide
The first house by the water-side,
Singing in her song she died,
    The Lady of Shalott.

Under tower and balcony,
By garden-wall and gallery,
A gleaming shape she floated by,
Dead-pale between the houses high,
    Silent into Camelot.
Out upon the wharfs they came,
Knight and burgher, lord and dame,
And round the prow they read her name,
    The Lady of Shalott.

130

140

150

160

24

Who is this? and what is here?
And in the lighted palace near
Died the sound of royal cheer;
And they cross'd themselves for fear,
      All the knights at Camelot:
But Lancelot mused a little space;
He said, 'She has a lovely face;
God in his mercy lend her grace,   70
      The Lady of Shalott.'

THE PALACE OF ART

I built my soul a lordly pleasure-house,
   Wherein at ease for aye to dwell.
I said, 'O Soul, make merry and carouse,
      Dear soul, for all is well.'

A huge crag-platform, smooth as burnish'd brass
   I chose. The ranged ramparts bright
From level meadow-bases of deep grass
      Suddenly scaled the light.

Thereon I built it firm. Of ledge or shelf
   The rock rose clear, or winding stair.   10
My soul would live alone unto herself
      In her high palace there.

And 'while the world runs round and round,' I said,
   'Reign thou apart, a quiet king,
Still as, while Saturn whirls, his stedfast shade
      Sleeps on his luminous ring.'

To which my soul made answer readily:
   'Trust me, in bliss I shall abide
In this great mansion, that is built for me,
      So royal-rich and wide.'

*   *   *

Four courts I made, East, West and South and North,
  In each a squared lawn, wherefrom
The golden gorge of dragons spouted forth
  A flood of fountain-foam.

And round the cool green courts there ran a row
  Of cloisters, branch'd like mighty woods,
Echoing all night to that sonorous flow
  Of spouted fountain-floods.

And round the roofs of gilded gallery
  That lent broad verge to distant lands,   30
Far as the wild swan wings, to where the sky
  Dipt down to sea and sands.

From those four jets four currents in one swell
  Across the mountain stream'd below
In misty folds, that floating as they fell
  Lit up a torrent-bow.

And high on every peak a statue seem'd
  To hang on tiptoe, tossing up
A cloud of incense of all odour steam'd
  From out a golden cup.   40

So that she thought, 'And who shall gaze upon
  My palace with unblinded eyes,
While this great bow will waver in the sun,
  And that sweet incense rise?'

For that sweet incense rose and never fail'd,
  And, while day sank or mounted higher,
The light aërial gallery, golden-rail'd,
  Burnt like a fringe of fire.

Likewise the deep-set windows, stain'd and traced,
  Would seem slow-flaming crimson fires   50
From shadow'd grots of arches interlaced,
  And tipt with frost-like spires.

* * *

Full of long-sounding corridors it was,
 That over-vaulted grateful gloom,
Thro' which the livelong day my soul did pass,
  Well-pleased, from room to room.

Full of great rooms and small the palace stood,
 All various, each a perfect whole
From living Nature, fit for every mood
  And change of my still soul.   60

For some were hung with arras green and blue,
 Showing a gaudy summer-morn,
Where with puff'd cheek the belted hunter blew
  His wreathed bugle-horn.

One seem'd all dark and red – a tract of sand,
 And some one pacing there alone,
Who paced for ever in a glimmering land,
  Lit with a low large moon.

One show'd an iron coast and angry waves.
 You seem'd to hear them climb and fall   70
And roar rock-thwarted under bellowing caves
  Beneath the windy wall.

And one, a full-fed river winding slow
 By herds upon an endless plain,
The ragged rims of thunder brooding low,
  With shadow-streaks of rain.

And one, the reapers at their sultry toil.
 In front they bound the sheaves. Behind
Were realms of upland, prodigal in oil,
  And hoary to the wind.   80

And one a foreground black with stones and slags,
 Beyond, a line of heights, and higher
All barr'd with long white cloud the scornful crags,
  And highest, snow and fire.

27

And one, an English home – gray twilight pour'd
   On dewy pastures, dewy trees,
Softer than sleep – all things in order stored,
     A haunt of ancient Peace.

Nor these alone, but every landscape fair,
   As fit for every mood of mind,   90
Or gay, or grave, or sweet, or stern, was there
     Not less than truth design'd.

      ★ ★ ★

Or the maid-mother by a crucifix,
   In tracts of pasture sunny-warm,
Beneath branch-work of costly sardonyx
     Sat smiling, babe in arm.

Or in a clear-wall'd city on the sea,
   Near gilded organ-pipes, her hair
Wound with white roses, slept St. Cecily;
     An angel look'd at her.   100

Or thronging all one porch of Paradise
   A group of Houris bow'd to see
The dying Islamite, with hands and eyes
     That said, We wait for thee.

Or mythic Uther's deeply-wounded son
   In some fair space of sloping greens
Lay, dozing in the vale of Avalon,
     And watch'd by weeping queens.

Or hollowing one hand against his ear,
   To list a foot-fall, ere he saw   110
The wood-nymph, stay'd the Ausonian king to hear
     Of wisdom and of law.

Or over hills with peaky tops engrail'd,
   And many a tract of palm and rice,
The throne of Indian Cama slowly sail'd
     A summer fann'd with spice.

Or sweet Europa's mantle blew unclasp'd,
    From off her shoulder backward borne:
From one hand droop'd a crocus: one hand grasp'd
      The mild bull's golden horn.   120

Or else flush'd Ganymede, his rosy thigh
    Half-buried in the Eagle's down,
Sole as a flying star shot thro' the sky
      Above the pillar'd town.

Nor these alone: but every legend fair
    Which the supreme Caucasian mind
Carved out of Nature for itself, was there,
      Not less than life, design'd.

            ★   ★   ★

Then in the towers I placed great bells that swung,
    Moved of themselves, with silver sound;   130
And with choice paintings of wise men I hung
      The royal dais round.

For there was Milton like a seraph strong,
    Beside him Shakespeare bland and mild;
And there the world-worn Dante grasp'd his song,
      And somewhat grimly smiled.

And there the Ionian father of the rest;
    A million wrinkles carved his skin;
A hundred winters snow'd upon his breast,
      From cheek and throat and chin.   140

Above, the fair hall-ceiling stately-set
    Many an arch high up did lift,
And angels rising and descending met
      With interchange of gift.

Below was all mosaic choicely plann'd
   With cycles of the human tale
Of this wide world, the times of every land
    So wrought, they will not fail.

The people here, a beast of burden slow,
   Toil'd onward, prick'd with goads and stings;   150
Here play'd, a tiger, rolling to and fro
    The heads and crowns of kings;

Here rose, an athlete, strong to break or bind
   All force in bonds that might endure,
And here once more like some sick man declined,
    And trusted any cure.

But over these she trod: and those great bells
   Began to chime. She took her throne:
She sat betwixt the shining Oriels,
    To sing her songs alone.   160

And thro' the topmost Oriels' coloured flame
   Two godlike faces gazed below;
Plato the wise, and large-brow'd Verulam,
    The first of those who know.

And all those names, that in their motion were
   Full-welling fountain-heads of change,
Betwixt the slender shafts were blazon'd fair
    In diverse raiment strange:

Thro' which the lights, rose, amber, emerald, blue,
   Flush'd in her temples and her eyes,   170
And from her lips, as morn from Memnon, drew
    Rivers of melodies.

No nightingale delighteth to prolong
   Her low preamble all alone,
More than my soul to hear her echo'd song
    Throb thro' the ribbed stone;

Singing and murmuring in her feastful mirth,
   Joying to feel herself alive,
Lord over Nature, Lord of the visible earth,
    Lord of the senses five;   180

Communing with herself: 'All these are mine,
   And let the world have peace or wars,
'Tis one to me.' She – when young night divine
    Crown'd dying day with stars,

Making sweet close of his delicious toils –
   Lit light in wreaths and anadems,
And pure quintessences of precious oils
    In hollow'd moons of gems,

To mimic heaven; and clapt her hands and cried,
   'I marvel if my still delight   190
In this great house so royal-rich, and wide,
    Be flatter'd to the height.

'O all things fair to sate my various eyes!
   O shapes and hues that please me well!
O silent faces of the Great and Wise,
    My Gods, with whom I dwell!

'O God-like isolation which art mine,
   I can but count thee perfect gain,
What time I watch the darkening droves of swine
    That range on yonder plain.   200

'In filthy sloughs they roll a prurient skin,
   They graze and wallow, breed and sleep;
And oft some brainless devil enters in,
    And drives them to the deep.'

Then of the moral instinct would she prate
   And of the rising from the dead,
As hers by right of full-accomplish'd Fate;
    And at the last she said:

'I take possession of man's mind and deed.
   I care not what the sects may brawl.   210
I sit as God holding no form of creed,
     But contemplating all.'

★ ★ ★

Full oft the riddle of the painful earth
   Flash'd thro' her as she sat alone,
Yet not the less held she her solemn mirth,
     And intellectual throne.

And so she throve and prosper'd: so three years
   She prosper'd: on the fourth she fell,
Like Herod, when the shout was in his ears,
     Struck thro' with pangs of hell.   220

Lest she should fail and perish utterly,
   God, before whom ever lie bare
The abysmal deeps of Personality,
     Plagued her with sore despair.

When she would think, where'er she turn'd her sight
   The airy hand confusion wrought,
Wrote, 'Mene, mene,' and divided quite
     The kingdom of her thought.

Deep dread and loathing of her solitude
   Fell on her, from which mood was born   230
Scorn of herself, again, from out that mood
     Laughter at her self-scorn.

'What! is not this my place of strength,' she said,
   'My spacious mansion built for me,
Whereof the strong foundation-stones were laid
     Since my first memory?'

But in dark corners of her palace stood
    Uncertain shapes; and unawares
On white-eyed phantasms weeping tears of blood,
    And horrible nightmares,   240

And hollow shades enclosing hearts of flame,
    And, with dim fretted foreheads all,
On corpses three-months-old at noon she came,
    That stood against the wall.

A spot of dull stagnation, without light
    Or power of movement, seem'd my soul,
'Mid onward-sloping motions infinite
    Making for one sure goal.

A still salt pool, lock'd in with bars of sand,
    Left on the shore; that hears all night   250
The plunging seas draw backward from the land
    Their moon-led waters white.

A star that with the choral starry dance
    Join'd not, but stood, and standing saw
The hollow orb of moving Circumstance
    Roll'd round by one fix'd law.

Back on herself her serpent pride had curl'd.
    'No voice,' she shriek'd in that lone hall,
'No voice breaks thro' the stillness of this world:
    One deep, deep silence all!'   260

She, mouldering with the dull earth's mouldering sod,
    Inwrapt tenfold in slothful shame,
Lay there exiled from eternal God,
    Lost to her place and name;

And death and life she hated equally,
    And nothing saw, for her despair,
But dreadful time, dreadful eternity,
    No comfort anywhere;

Remaining utterly confused with fears,
   And ever worse with growing time,
And ever unrelieved by dismal tears,   270
    And all alone in crime:

Shut up as in a crumbling tomb, girt round
   With blackness as a solid wall,
Far off she seem'd to hear the dully sound
    Of human footsteps fall.

As in strange lands a traveller walking slow,
   In doubt and great perplexity,
A little before moon-rise hears the low
    Moan of an unknown sea;   280

And knows not if it be thunder, or a sound
   Of rocks thrown down, or one deep cry
Of great wild beasts; then thinketh, 'I have found
    A new land, but I die.'

She howl'd aloud, 'I am on fire within.
   There comes no murmur of reply.
What is it that will take away my sin,
    And save me lest I die?'

So when four years were wholly finished
   She threw her royal robes away.   290
'Make me a cottage in the vale,' she said,
    'Where I may mourn and pray.

'Yet pull not down my palace towers, that are
   So lightly, beautifully built:
Perchance I may return with others there
    When I have purged my guilt.'

THE LOTOS-EATERS

'Courage!' he said, and pointed toward the land,
'This mounting wave will roll us shoreward soon.'
In the afternoon they came unto a land
In which it seemed always afternoon.
All round the coast the languid air did swoon,
Breathing like one that hath a weary dream.
Full-faced above the valley stood the moon;
And like a downward smoke, the slender stream
Along the cliff to fall and pause and fall did seem.

A land of streams! some, like a downward smoke,   10
Slow-dropping veils of thinnest lawn, did go;
And some thro' wavering lights and shadows broke,
Rolling a slumbrous sheet of foam below.
They saw the gleaming river seaward flow
From the inner land: far off, three mountain-tops,
Three silent pinnacles of aged snow,
Stood sunset-flush'd: and, dew'd with showery drops,
Up-clomb the shadowy pine above the woven copse.

The charmed sunset linger'd low adown
In the red West: thro' mountain clefts the dale   20
Was seen far inland, and the yellow down
Border'd with palm, and many a winding vale
And meadow, set with slender galingale;
A land where all things always seem'd the same!
And round about the keel with faces pale,
Dark faces pale against that rosy flame,
The mild-eyed melancholy Lotos-eaters came.

Branches they bore of that enchanted stem,
Laden with flower and fruit, whereof they gave
To each, but whoso did receive of them,   30
And taste, to him the gushing of the wave
Far far away did seem to mourn and rave
On alien shores; and if his fellow spake,
His voice was thin, as voices from the grave;
And deep-asleep he seem'd, yet all awake,
And music in his ears his beating heart did make.

35

They sat them down upon the yellow sand,
Between the sun and moon upon the shore;
And sweet it was to dream of Fatherland,
Of child, and wife, and slave; but evermore
Most weary seem'd the sea, weary the oar,
Weary the wandering fields of barren foam.
Then some one said, 'We will return no more;'
And all at once they sang, 'Our island home
Is far beyond the wave; we will no longer roam.'

Choric Song

I

There is sweet music here that softer falls
Than petals from blown roses on the grass,
Or night-dews on still waters between walls
Of shadowy granite, in a gleaming pass;
Music that gentlier on the spirit lies,   50
Than tir'd eyelids upon tir'd eyes;
Music that brings sweet sleep down from the blissful skies.
Here are cool mosses deep,
And thro' the moss the ivies creep,
And in the stream the long-leaved flowers weep,
And from the craggy ledge the poppy hangs in sleep.

II

Why are we weigh'd upon with heaviness,
And utterly consumed with sharp distress,
While all things else have rest from weariness?
All things have rest: why should we toil alone,   60
We only toil, who are the first of things,
And make perpetual moan,
Still from one sorrow to another thrown:
Nor ever fold our wings,
And cease from wanderings,
Nor steep our brows in slumber's holy balm;
Nor harken what the inner spirit sings,
'There is no joy but calm!'
Why should we only toil, the roof and crown of things?

III

Lo! in the middle of the wood,   70
The folded leaf is woo'd from out the bud
With winds upon the branch, and there
Grows green and broad, and takes no care,
Sun-steep'd at noon, and in the moon
Nightly dew-fed; and turning yellow
Falls, and floats adown the air.
Lo! sweeten'd with the summer light,
The full-juiced apple, waxing over-mellow,
Drops in a silent autumn night.
All its allotted length of days,   80
The flower ripens in its place,
Ripens and fades, and falls, and hath no toil,
Fast-rooted in the fruitful soil.

IV

Hateful is the dark-blue sky,
Vaulted o'er the dark-blue sea.
Death is the end of life; ah, why
Should life all labour be?
Let us alone. Time driveth onward fast,
And in a little while our lips are dumb.
Let us alone. What is it that will last?   90
All things are taken from us, and become
Portions and parcels of the dreadful Past.
Let us alone. What pleasure can we have
To war with evil? Is there any peace
In ever climbing up the climbing wave?
All things have rest, and ripen toward the grave
In silence; ripen, fall and cease:
Give us long rest or death, dark death, or dreamful ease.

V

How sweet it were, hearing the downward stream,
With half-shut eyes ever to seem   100
Falling asleep in a half-dream!
To dream and dream, like yonder amber light,

Which will not leave the myrrh-bush on the height;
To hear each other's whisper'd speech;
Eating the Lotos day by day,
To watch the crisping ripples on the beach,
And tender curving lines of creamy spray;
To lend our hearts and spirits wholly
To the influence of mild-minded melancholy;
To muse and brood and live again in memory,   110
With those old faces of our infancy
Heap'd over with a mound of grass,
Two handfuls of white dust, shut in an urn of brass!

VI

Dear is the memory of our wedded lives,
And dear the last embraces of our wives
And their warm tears: but all hath suffer'd change:
For surely now our household hearths are cold:
Our sons inherit us: our looks are strange:
And we should come like ghosts to trouble joy.
Or else the island princes over-bold   120
Have eat our substance, and the minstrel sings
Before them of the ten years' war in Troy,
And our great deeds, as half-forgotten things.
Is there confusion in the little isle?
Let what is broken so remain.
The Gods are hard to reconcile:
'Tis hard to settle order once again.
There *is* confusion worse than death,
Trouble on trouble, pain on pain,
Long labour unto aged breath,
Sore task to hearts worn out by many wars
And eyes grown dim with gazing on the pilot-stars.

VII

But, propt on beds of amaranth and moly,
How sweet (while warm airs lull us, blowing lowly)
With half-dropt eyelid still,
Beneath a heaven dark and holy,
To watch the long bright river drawing slowly

His waters from the purple hill –
To hear the dewy echoes calling
From cave to cave thro' the thick-twined vine –
To watch the emerald-colour'd water falling
Thro' many a wov'n acanthus-wreath divine!
Only to hear and see the far-off sparkling brine,
Only to hear were sweet, stretch'd out beneath the pine.

VIII

The Lotos blooms below the barren peak:
The Lotos blows by every winding creek:
All day the wind breathes low with mellower tone:
Thro' every hollow cave and alley lone
Round and round the spicy downs the yellow Lotos-dust is
    blown.
We have had enough of action, and of motion we,
Roll'd to starboard, roll'd to larboard, when the surge was
    seething free,
Where the wallowing monster spouted his foam-fountains in the
    sea.
Let us swear an oath, and keep it with an equal mind,
In the hollow Lotos-land to live and lie reclined
On the hills like Gods together, careless of mankind.
For they lie beside their nectar, and the bolts are hurl'd
Far below them in the valleys, and the clouds are lightly curl'd
Round their golden houses, girdled with the gleaming world:
Where they smile in secret, looking over wasted lands,
Blight and famine, plague and earthquake, roaring deeps and fiery
    sands,
Clanging fights, and flaming towns, and sinking ships, and praying
    hands.
But they smile, they find a music centred in a doleful song
Steaming up, a lamentation and an ancient tale of wrong,
Like a tale of little meaning tho' the words are strong;
Chanted from an ill-used race of men that cleave the soil,
Sow the seed, and reap the harvest with enduring toil,
Storing yearly little dues of wheat, and wine and oil;
Till they perish and they suffer – some, 'tis whisper'd – down in
    hell

Suffer endless anguish, others in Elysian valleys dwell,
Resting weary limbs at last on beds of asphodel.
Surely, surely, slumber is more sweet than toil, the shore
Than labour in the deep mid-ocean, wind and wave and oar;
Oh rest ye, brother mariners, we will not wander more.

THE GARDENER'S DAUGHTER;

or, The Pictures

This morning is the morning of the day,
When I and Eustace from the city went
To see the Gardener's Daughter; I and he,
Brothers in Art; a friendship so complete
Portion'd in halves between us, that we grew
The fable of the city where we dwelt.

   My Eustace might have sat for Hercules;
So muscular he spread, so broad of breast.
He, by some law that holds in love, and draws
The greater to the lesser, long desired   10
A certain miracle of symmetry,
A miniature of loveliness, all grace
Summ'd up and closed in little; – Juliet, she
So light of foot, so light of spirit – oh, she
To me myself, for some three careless moons,
The summer pilot of an empty heart
Unto the shores of nothing! Know you not
Such touches are but embassies of love,
To tamper with the feelings, ere he found
Empire for life? but Eustace painted her,   20
And said to me, she sitting with us then,
'When will *you* paint like this?' and I replied,
(My words were half in earnest, half in jest,)
''Tis not your work, but Love's. Love, unperceived,
A more ideal Artist he than all,
Came, drew your pencil from you, made those eyes
Darker than darkest pansies, and that hair
More black than ashbuds in the front of March.'
And Juliet answer'd laughing, 'Go and see

40

The Gardener's daughter: trust me, after that,   30
You scarce can fail to match his masterpiece.'
And up we rose, and on the spur we went.

  Not wholly in the busy world, nor quite
Beyond it, blooms the garden that I love.
News from the humming city comes to it
In sound of funeral or of marriage bells;
And, sitting muffled in dark leaves, you hear
The windy clanging of the minster clock;
Although between it and the garden lies
A league of grass, wash'd by a slow broad stream,   40
That, stirr'd with languid pulses of the oar,
Waves all its lazy lilies, and creeps on,
Barge-laden, to three arches of a bridge
Crown'd with the minster-towers.
                              The fields between
Are dewy-fresh, browsed by deep-udder'd kine,
And all about the large lime feathers low,
The lime a summer home of murmurous wings.

  In that still place she, hoarded in herself,
Grew, seldom seen; not less among us lived
Her fame from lip to lip. Who had not heard   50
Of Rose, the Gardener's daughter? Where was he,
So blunt in memory, so old at heart,
At such a distance from his youth in grief,
That, having seen, forgot? The common mouth,
So gross to express delight, in praise of her
Grew oratory. Such a lord is Love,
And Beauty such a mistress of the world.

  And if I said that Fancy, led by Love,
Would play with flying forms and images,
Yet this is also true, that, long before   60
I look'd upon her, when I heard her name
My heart was like a prophet to my heart,
And told me I should love. A crowd of hopes,
That sought to sow themselves like winged seeds,

Born out of everything I heard and saw,
Flutter'd about my senses and my soul;
And vague desires, like fitful blasts of balm
To one that travels quickly, made the air
Of Life delicious, and all kinds of thought,
That verged upon them, sweeter than the dream   70
Dream'd by a happy man, when the dark East,
Unseen, is brightening to his bridal morn.

   And sure this orbit of the memory folds
For ever in itself the day we went
To see her. All the land in flowery squares,
Beneath a broad and equal-blowing wind,
Smelt of the coming summer, as one large cloud
Drew downward: but all else of heaven was pure
Up to the Sun, and May from verge to verge,
And May with me from head to heel. And now,   80
As tho' 'twere yesterday, as tho' it were
The hour just flown, that morn with all its sound,
(For those old Mays had thrice the life of these,)
Rings in mine ears. The steer forgot to graze,
And, where the hedge-row cuts the pathway, stood,
Leaning his horns into the neighbour field,
And lowing to his fellows. From the woods
Came voices of the well-contented doves.
The lark could scarce get out his notes for joy,
But shook his song together as he near'd   90
His happy home, the ground. To left and right,
The cuckoo told his name to all the hills;
The mellow ouzel fluted in the elm;
The redcap whistled; and the nightingale
Sang loud, as tho' he were the bird of day.

   And Eustace turn'd, and smiling said to me,
'Hear how the bushes echo! by my life,
These birds have joyful thoughts. Think you they sing
Like poets, from the vanity of song?
Or have they any sense of why they sing?   100
And would they praise the heavens for what they have?'

And I made answer, 'Were there nothing else
For which to praise the heavens but only love,
That only love were cause enough for praise.'

  Lightly he laugh'd, as one that read my thought,
And on we went; but ere an hour had pass'd,
We reach'd a meadow slanting to the North;
Down which a well-worn pathway courted us
To one green wicket in a privet hedge;
This, yielding, gave into a grassy walk   110
Thro' crowded lilac-ambush trimly pruned;
And one warm gust, full-fed with perfume, blew
Beyond us, as we enter'd in the cool.
The garden stretches southward. In the midst
A cedar spread his dark-green layers of shade.
The garden-glasses glanced, and momently
The twinkling laurel scatter'd silver lights.

  'Eustace,' I said, 'this wonder keeps the house.'
He nodded, but a moment afterwards
He cried, 'Look! look!' Before he ceased I turn'd,   120
And, ere a star can wink, beheld her there.

  For up the porch there grew an Eastern rose,
That, flowering high, the last night's gale had caught,
And blown across the walk. One arm aloft –
Gown'd in pure white, that fitted to the shape –
Holding the bush, to fix it back, she stood,
A single stream of all her soft brown hair
Pour'd on one side: the shadow of the flowers
Stole all the golden gloss, and, wavering
Lovingly lower, trembled on her waist –   130
Ah, happy shade – and still went wavering down,
But, ere it touch'd a foot, that might have danced
The greensward into greener circles, dipt,
And mix'd with shadows of the common ground!
But the full day dwelt on her brows, and sunn'd
Her violet eyes, and all her Hebe bloom,
And doubled his own warmth against her lips,

43

And on the bounteous wave of such a breast
As never pencil drew. Half light, half shade,
She stood, a sight to make an old man young.   140

    So rapt, we near'd the house; but she, a Rose
In roses, mingled with her fragrant toil,
Nor heard us come, nor from her tendance turn'd
Into the world without; till close at hand,
And almost ere I knew mine own intent,
This murmur broke the stillness of that air
Which brooded round about her:
                                    'Ah, one rose,
One rose, but one, by those fair fingers cull'd,
Were worth a hundred kisses press'd on lips
Less exquisite than thine.'
                            She look'd: but all   150
Suffused with blushes − neither self-possess'd
Nor startled, but betwixt this mood and that,
Divided in a graceful quiet − paused,
And dropt the branch she held, and turning, wound
Her looser hair in braid, and stirr'd her lips
For some sweet answer, tho' no answer came,
Nor yet refused the rose, but granted it,
And moved away, and left me, statue-like,
In act to render thanks.
                            I, that whole day,
Saw her no more, altho' I linger'd there   160
Till every daisy slept, and Love's white star
Beam'd thro' the thicken'd cedar in the dusk.

    So home we went, and all the livelong way
With solemn gibe did Eustace banter me.
'Now,' said he, 'will you climb the top of Art.
You cannot fail but work in hues to dim
The Titianic Flora. Will you match
My Juliet? you, not you, − the Master, Love,
A more ideal Artist he than all.'

So home I went, but could not sleep for joy,   170
Reading her perfect features in the gloom,
Kissing the rose she gave me o'er and o'er,
And shaping faithful record of the glance
That graced the giving – such a noise of life
Swarm'd in the golden present, such a voice
Call'd to me from the years to come, and such
A length of bright horizon rimm'd the dark.
And all that night I heard the watchman peal
The sliding season: all that night I heard
The heavy clocks knolling the drowsy hours.   180
The drowsy hours, dispensers of all good,
O'er the mute city stole with folded wings,
Distilling odours on me as they went
To greet their fairer sisters of the East.

Love at first sight, first-born, and heir to all,
Made this night thus. Henceforward squall nor storm
Could keep me from that Eden where she dwelt.
Light pretexts drew me; sometimes a Dutch love
For tulips; then for roses, moss or musk,
To grace my city rooms; or fruits and cream   190
Served in the weeping elm; and more and more
A word could bring the colour to my cheek;
A thought would fill my eyes with happy dew;
Love trebled life within me, and with each
The year increased.
                    The daughters of the year,
One after one, thro' that still garden pass'd;
Each garlanded with her peculiar flower
Danced into light, and died into the shade;
And each in passing touch'd with some new grace
Or seem'd to touch her, so that day by day,   200
Like one that never can be wholly known,
Her beauty grew; till Autumn brought an hour
For Eustace, when I heard his deep 'I will,'
Breathed, like the covenant of a God, to hold
From thence thro' all the worlds: but I rose up
Full of his bliss, and following her dark eyes

45

Felt earth as air beneath me, till I reach'd
The wicket-gate, and found her standing there.

There sat we down upon a garden mound,
Two mutually enfolded; Love, the third,   210
Between us, in the circle of his arms
Enwound us both; and over many a range
Of waning lime the gray cathedral towers,
Across a hazy glimmer of the west,
Reveal'd their shining windows: from them clash'd
The bells; we listen'd; with the time we play'd,
We spoke of other things; we coursed about
The subject most at heart, more near and near,
Like doves about a dovecote, wheeling round
The central wish, until we settled there.   220

Then, in that time and place, I spoke to her,
Requiring, tho' I knew it was mine own,
Yet for the pleasure that I took to hear,
Requiring at her hand the greatest gift,
A woman's heart, the heart of her I loved;
And in that time and place she answer'd me,
And in the compass of three little words,
More musical than ever came in one,
The silver fragments of a broken voice,
Made me most happy, faltering, 'I am thine.'   230

Shall I cease here? Is this enough to say
That my desire, like all strongest hopes,
By its own energy fulfill'd itself,
Merged in completion? Would you learn at full
How passion rose thro' circumstantial grades
Beyond all grades develop'd? and indeed
I had not staid so long to tell you all,
But while I mused came Memory with sad eyes,
Holding the folded annals of my youth;
And while I mused, Love with knit brows went by,   240
And with a flying finger swept my lips,
And spake, 'Be wise: not easily forgiven

Are those, who setting wide the doors that bar
The secret bridal-chambers of the heart,
Let in the day.' Here, then, my words have end.

Yet might I tell of meetings, of farewells –
Of that which came between, more sweet than each,
In whispers, like the whispers of the leaves
That tremble round a nightingale – in sighs
Which perfect Joy, perplex'd for utterance,   250
Stole from her sister Sorrow. Might I not tell
Of difference, reconcilement, pledges given,
And vows, where there was never need of vows,
And kisses, where the heart on one wild leap
Hung tranced from all pulsation, as above
The heavens between their fairy fleeces pale
Sow'd all their mystic gulfs with fleeting stars;
Or while the balmy glooming, crescent-lit,
Spread the light haze along the river-shores,
And in the hollows; or as once we met   260
Unheedful, tho' beneath a whispering rain
Night slid down one long stream of sighing wind,
And in her bosom bore the baby, Sleep.

But this whole hour your eyes have been intent
On that veil'd picture – veil'd, for what it holds
May not be dwelt on by the common day.
This prelude has prepared thee. Raise thy soul;
Make thine heart ready with thine eyes: the time
Is come to raise the veil.
                              Behold her there,
As I beheld her ere she knew my heart,   270
My first, last love; the idol of my youth,
The darling of my manhood, and, alas!
Now the most blessed memory of mine age.

THE TWO VOICES

A still small voice spake unto me,
'Thou art so full of misery,
Were it not better not to be?'

Then to the still small voice I said;
'Let me not cast in endless shade
What is so wonderfully made.'

To which the voice did urge reply;
'To-day I saw the dragon-fly
Come from the wells where he did lie.

'An inner impulse rent the veil   10
Of his old husk: from head to tail
Came out clear plates of sapphire mail.

'He dried his wings: like gauze they grew;
Thro' crofts and pastures wet with dew
A living flash of light he flew.'

I said, 'When first the world began,
Young Nature thro' five cycles ran,
And in the sixth she moulded man.

'She gave him mind, the lordliest
Proportion, and, above the rest,   20
Dominion in the head and breast.'

Thereto the silent voice replied;
'Self-blinded are you by your pride;
Look up thro' night: the world is wide.

'This truth within thy mind rehearse,
That in a boundless universe
Is boundless better, boundless worse.

'Think you this mould of hopes and fears
Could find no statelier than his peers
In yonder hundred million spheres?'   30

It spake, moreover, in my mind:
'Tho' thou wert scatter'd to the wind,
Yet is there plenty of the kind.'

Then did my response clearer fall:
'No compound of this earthly ball
Is like another, all in all.'

To which he answer'd scoffingly;
'Good soul! suppose I grant it thee,
Who'll weep for thy deficiency?

'Or will one beam be less intense,   40
When thy peculiar difference
Is cancell'd in the world of sense?'

I would have said, 'Thou canst not know,'
But my full heart, that work'd below,
Rain'd thro' my sight its overflow.

Again the voice spake unto me:
'Thou art so steep'd in misery,
Surely 'twere better not to be.

'Thine anguish will not let thee sleep,
Nor any train of reason keep: 50
Thou canst not think, but thou wilt weep.'

I said, 'The years with change advance:
If I make dark my countenance,
I shut my life from happier chance.

'Some turn this sickness yet might take,
Ev'n yet.' But he: 'What drug can make
A wither'd palsy cease to shake?'

I wept, 'Tho' I should die, I know
That all about the thorn will blow
In tufts of rosy-tinted snow;   60

'And men, thro' novel spheres of thought
Still moving after truth long sought,
Will learn new things when I am not.'

'Yet,' said the secret voice, 'some time,
Sooner or later, will gray prime
Make thy grass hoar with early rime.

'Not less swift souls that yearn for light,
Rapt after heaven's starry flight,
Would sweep the tracts of day and night.

'Not less the bee would range her cells,   70
The furzy prickle fire the dells,
The foxglove cluster dappled bells.'

I said that 'all the years invent;
Each month is various to present
The world with some development.

'Were this not well, to bide mine hour,
Tho' watching from a ruin'd tower
How grows the day of human power?'

'The highest-mounted mind,' he said,
'Still sees the sacred morning spread   80
The silent summit overhead.

'Will thirty seasons render plain
Those lonely lights that still remain,
Just breaking over land and main?

'Or make that morn, from his cold crown
And crystal silence creeping down,
Flood with full daylight glebe and town?

'Forerun thy peers, thy time, and let
Thy feet, millenniums hence, be set
In midst of knowledge, dream'd not yet.   90

'Thou hast not gain'd a real height,
Nor art thou nearer to the light,
Because the scale is infinite.

''Twere better not to breathe or speak,
Than cry for strength, remaining weak,
And seem to find, but still to seek.

'Moreover, but to seem to find
Asks what thou lackest, thought resign'd,
A healthy frame, a quiet mind.'

I said, 'When I am gone away,   100
"He dared not tarry," men will say,
Doing dishonour to my clay.'

'This is more vile,' he made reply,
'To breathe and loathe, to live and sigh,
Than once from dread of pain to die.

'Sick art thou – a divided will
Still heaping on the fear of ill
The fear of men, a coward still.

'Do men love thee? Art thou so bound
To men, that how thy name may sound   110
Will vex thee lying underground?

'The memory of the wither'd leaf
In endless time is scarce more brief
Than of the garner'd Autumn-sheaf.

'Go, vexed Spirit, sleep in trust;
The right ear, that is fill'd with dust,
Hears little of the false or just.'

'Hard task, to pluck resolve,' I cried,
'From emptiness and the waste wide
Of that abyss, or scornful pride!   120

'Nay – rather yet that I could raise
One hope that warm'd me in the days
While still I yearn'd for human praise.

'When, wide in soul and bold of tongue,
Among the tents I paused and sung,
The distant battle flash'd and rung.

'I sung the joyful Pæan clear,
And, sitting, burnish'd without fear
The brand, the buckler, and the spear –

'Waiting to strive a happy strife,   130
To war with falsehood to the knife,
And not to lose the good of life –

'Some hidden principle to move,
To put together, part and prove,
And mete the bounds of hate and love –

'As far as might be, to carve out
Free space for every human doubt,
That the whole mind might orb about –

'To search thro' all I felt or saw,
The springs of life, the depths of awe,   140
And reach the law within the law:

'At least, not rotting like a weed,
But, having sown some generous seed,
Fruitful of further thought and deed,

'To pass, when Life her light withdraws,
Not void of righteous self-applause,
Nor in a merely selfish cause –

'In some good cause, not in mine own,
To perish, wept for, honour'd, known,
And like a warrior overthrown;   150

'Whose eyes are dim with glorious tears,
When, soil'd with noble dust, he hears
His country's war-song thrill his ears:

'Then dying of a mortal stroke,
What time the foeman's line is broke,
And all the war is roll'd in smoke.'

'Yea!' said the voice, 'thy dream was good,
While thou abodest in the bud.
It was the stirring of the blood.

'If Nature put not forth her power   160
About the opening of the flower,
Who is it that could live an hour?

'Then comes the check, the change, the fall,
Pain rises up, old pleasures pall.
There is one remedy for all.

'Yet hadst thou, thro' enduring pain,
Link'd month to month with such a chain
Of knitted purport, all were vain.

'Thou hadst not between death and birth
Dissolved the riddle of the earth.   170
So were thy labour little-worth.

'That men with knowledge merely play'd,
I told thee – hardly nigher made,
Tho' scaling slow from grade to grade;

'Much less this dreamer, deaf and blind,
Named man, may hope some truth to find,
That bears relation to the mind.

'For every worm beneath the moon
Draws different threads, and late and soon
Spins, toiling out his own cocoon.   180

'Cry, faint not: either Truth is born
Beyond the polar gleam forlorn,
Or in the gateways of the morn.

'Cry, faint not, climb: the summits slope
Beyond the furthest flights of hope,
Wrapt in dense cloud from base to cope.

'Sometimes a little corner shines,
As over rainy mist inclines
A gleaming crag with belts of pines.

'I will go forward, sayest thou,   190
I shall not fail to find her now.
Look up, the fold is on her brow.

'If straight thy track, or if oblique,
Thou know'st not. Shadows thou dost strike,
Embracing cloud, Ixion-like;

'And owning but a little more
Than beasts, abidest lame and poor,
Calling thyself a little lower

'Than angels. Cease to wail and brawl!
Why inch by inch to darkness crawl?   200
There is one remedy for all.'

'O dull, one-sided voice,' said I,
'Wilt thou make everything a lie,
To flatter me that I may die?

'I know that age to age succeeds,
Blowing a noise of tongues and deeds,
A dust of systems and of creeds.

'I cannot hide that some have striven,
Achieving calm, to whom was given
The joy that mixes man with Heaven: 210

'Who, rowing hard against the stream,
Saw distant gates of Eden gleam,
And did not dream it was a dream;

'But heard, by secret transport led,
Ev'n in the charnels of the dead,
The murmur of the fountain-head –

'Which did accomplish their desire,
Bore and forbore, and did not tire,
Like Stephen, an unquenched fire.

'He heeded not reviling tones,   220
Nor sold his heart to idle moans,
Tho' cursed and scorn'd, and bruised with stones:

'But looking upward, full of grace,
He pray'd, and from a happy place
God's glory smote him on the face.'

The sullen answer slid betwixt:
'Not that the grounds of hope were fix'd,
The elements were kindlier mix'd.'

I said, 'I toil beneath the curse,
But, knowing not the universe,   230
I fear to slide from bad to worse.

'And that, in seeking to undo
One riddle, and to find the true,
I knit a hundred others new:

'Or that this anguish fleeting hence,
Unmanacled from bonds of sense,
Be fix'd and froz'n to permanence:

'For I go, weak from suffering here:
Naked I go, and void of cheer:
What is it that I may not fear?'   240

'Consider well,' the voice replied,
'His face, that two hours since hath died;
Wilt thou find passion, pain or pride?

'Will he obey when one commands?
Or answer should one press his hands?
He answers not, nor understands.

'His palms are folded on his breast:
There is no other thing express'd
But long disquiet merged in rest.

'His lips are very mild and meek: 250
Tho' one should smite him on the cheek,
And on the mouth, he will not speak.

'His little daughter, whose sweet face
He kiss'd, taking his last embrace,
Becomes dishonour to her race –

'His sons grow up that bear his name,
Some grow to honour, some to shame, –
But he is chill to praise or blame.

'He will not hear the north-wind rave,
Nor, moaning, household shelter crave   260
From winter rains that beat his grave.

'High up the vapours fold and swim:
About him broods the twilight dim:
The place he knew forgetteth him.'

'If all be dark, vague voice,' I said,
'These things are wrapt in doubt and dread,
Nor canst thou show the dead are dead.

'The sap dries up: the plant declines.
A deeper tale my heart divines.
Know I not Death? the outward signs?   270

'I found him when my years were few;
A shadow on the graves I knew,
And darkness in the village yew.

'From grave to grave the shadow crept:
In her still place the morning wept:
Touch'd by his feet the daisy slept.

'The simple senses crown'd his head:
"Omega! thou art Lord," they said,
"We find no motion in the dead."

'Why, if man rot in dreamless ease,   280
Should that plain fact, as taught by these,
Not make him sure that he shall cease?

'Who forged that other influence,
That heat of inward evidence,
By which he doubts against the sense?

'He owns the fatal gift of eyes,
That read his spirit blindly wise,
Not simple as a thing that dies.

'Here sits he shaping wings to fly:
His heart forebodes a mystery: 290
He names the name Eternity.

'That type of Perfect in his mind
In Nature can he nowhere find.
He sows himself on every wind.

'He seems to hear a Heavenly Friend,
And thro' thick veils to apprehend
A labour working to an end.

57

'The end and the beginning vex
His reason: many things perplex,
With motions, checks, and counterchecks.   300

He knows a baseness in his blood
At such strange war with something good,
He may not do the thing he would.

'Heaven opens inward, chasms yawn,
Vast images in glimmering dawn,
Half shown, are broken and withdrawn.

'Ah! sure within him and without,
Could his dark wisdom find it out,
There must be answer to his doubt,

'But thou canst answer not again.   310
With thine own weapon art thou slain,
Or thou wilt answer but in vain.

'The doubt would rest, I dare not solve.
In the same circle we revolve.
Assurance only breeds resolve.'

As when a billow, blown against,
Falls back, the voice with which I fenced
A little ceased, but recommenced.

'Where wert thou when thy father play'd
In his free field, and pastime made,   320
A merry boy in sun and shade?

'A merry boy they call'd him then,
He sat upon the knees of men
In days that never come again.

'Before the little ducts began
To feed thy bones with lime, and ran
Their course, till thou wert also man:

'Who took a wife, who rear'd his race,
Whose wrinkles gather'd on his face,
Whose troubles number with his days: 330

'A life of nothings, nothing-worth,
From that first nothing ere his birth
To that last nothing under earth!'

'These words,' I said, 'are like the rest;
No certain clearness, but at best
A vague suspicion of the breast:

'But if I grant, thou mightst defend
The thesis which thy words intend –
That to begin implies to end;

'Yet how should I for certain hold,   340
Because my memory is so cold,
That I first was in human mould?

'I cannot make this matter plain,
But I would shoot, howe'er in vain,
A random arrow from the brain.

'It may be that no life is found,
Which only to one engine bound
Falls off, but cycles always round.

'As old mythologies relate,
Some draught of Lethe might await   350
The slipping thro' from state to state.

'As here we find in trances, men
Forget the dream that happens then,
Until they fall in trance again.

'So might we, if our state were such
As one before, remember much,
For those two likes might meet and touch.

'But, if I lapsed from nobler place,
Some legend of a fallen race
Alone might hint of my disgrace;   360

'Some vague emotion of delight
In gazing up an Alpine height,
Some yearning toward the lamps of night;

'Or if thro' lower lives I came –
Tho' all experience past became
Consolidate in mind and frame –

'I might forget my weaker lot;
For is not our first year forgot?
The haunts of memory echo not.

'And men, whose reason long was blind,   370
From cells of madness unconfined,
Oft lose whole years of darker mind.

'Much more, if first I floated free,
As naked essence, must I be
Incompetent of memory:

'For memory dealing but with time,
And he with matter, could she climb
Beyond her own material prime?

'Moreover, something is or seems,
That touches me with mystic gleams,   380
Like glimpses of forgotten dreams –

'Of something felt, like something here;
Of something done, I know not where;
Such as no language may declare.'

The still voice laugh'd. 'I talk,' said he,
'Not with thy dreams. Suffice it thee
Thy pain is a reality.'

'But thou,' said I, 'hast missed thy mark,
Who sought'st to wreck my mortal ark,
By making all the horizon dark.   390

'Why not set forth, if I should do
This rashness, that which might ensue
With this old soul in organs new?

'Whatever crazy sorrow saith,
No life that breathes with human breath
Has ever truly long'd for death.

''Tis life, whereof our nerves are scant,
Oh life, not death, for which we pant;
More life, and fuller, that I want.'

I ceased, and sat as one forlorn.   400
Then said the voice, in quiet scorn,
'Behold, it is the Sabbath morn.'

And I arose, and I released
The casement, and the light increased
With freshness in the dawning east.

Like soften'd airs that blowing steal,
When meres begin to uncongeal,
The sweet church bells began to peal.

On to God's house the people prest:
Passing the place where each must rest,   410
Each enter'd like a welcome guest.

One walk'd between his wife and child,
With measured footfall firm and mild,
And now and then he gravely smiled.

The prudent partner of his blood
Lean'd on him, faithful, gentle, good,
Wearing the rose of womanhood.

And in their double love secure,
The little maiden walk'd demure,
Pacing with downward eyelids pure.   420

These three made unity so sweet,
My frozen heart began to beat,
Remembering its ancient heat.

I blest them, and they wander'd on:
I spoke, but answer came there none:
The dull and bitter voice was gone.

A second voice was at mine ear,
A little whisper silver-clear,
A murmur, 'Be of better cheer.'

As from some blissful neighbourhood,   430
A notice faintly understood,
'I see the end, and know the good.'

A little hint to solace woe,
A hint, a whisper breathing low,
'I may not speak of what I know.'

Like an Æolian harp that wakes
No certain air, but overtakes
Far thought with music that it makes:

Such seem'd the whisper at my side:
'What is it thou knowest, sweet voice?' I cried.   440
'A hidden hope,' the voice replied:

So heavenly-toned, that in that hour
From out my sullen heart a power
Broke, like the rainbow from the shower,

To feel, altho' no tongue can prove,
That every cloud, that spreads above
And veileth love, itself is love.

And forth into the fields I went,
And Nature's living motion lent
The pulse of hope to discontent.   450

I wonder'd at the bounteous hours,
The slow result of winter showers:
You scarce could see the grass for flowers.

I wonder'd, while I paced along:
The woods were fill'd so full with song,
There seem'd no room for sense of wrong;

And all so variously wrought,
I marvell'd how the mind was brought
To anchor by one gloomy thought;

And wherefore rather I made choice   460
To commune with that barren voice,
Than him that said, 'Rejoice! Rejoice!'

ST SIMEON STYLITES

Altho' I be the basest of mankind,
From scalp to sole one slough and crust of sin,
Unfit for earth, unfit for heaven, scarce meet
For troops of devils, mad with blasphemy,
I will not cease to grasp the hope I hold
Of saintdom, and to clamour, mourn and sob,
Battering the gates of heaven with storms of prayer,
Have mercy, Lord, and take away my sin.

   Let this avail, just, dreadful, mighty God,
This not be all in vain, that thrice ten years,   10
Thrice multiplied by superhuman pangs,
In hungers and in thirsts, fevers and cold,
In coughs, aches, stitches, ulcerous throes and cramps,
A sign betwixt the meadow and the cloud,
Patient on this tall pillar I have borne
Rain, wind, frost, heat, hail, damp, and sleet, and snow;

63

And I had hoped that ere this period closed
Thou wouldst have caught me up into thy rest,
Denying not these weather-beaten limbs
The meed of saints, the white robe and the palm.   20

  O take the meaning, Lord: I do not breathe,
Not whisper, any murmur of complaint.
Pain heap'd ten-hundred-fold to this, were still
Less burthen, by ten-hundred-fold, to bear,
Than were those lead-like tons of sin that crush'd
My spirit flat before thee.
               O Lord, Lord,
Thou knowest I bore this better at the first,
For I was strong and hale of body then;
And tho' my teeth, which now are dropt away,
Would chatter with the cold, and all my beard   30
Was tagg'd with icy fringes in the moon,
I drown'd the whoopings of the owl with sound
Of pious hymns and psalms, and sometimes saw
An angel stand and watch me, as I sang.
Now am I feeble grown; my end draws nigh;
I hope my end draws nigh: half deaf I am,
So that I scarce can hear the people hum
About the column's base, and almost blind,
And scarce can recognise the fields I know;
And both my thighs are rotted with the dew;   40
Yet cease I not to clamour and to cry,
While my stiff spine can hold my weary head,
Till all my limbs drop piecemeal from the stone,
Have mercy, mercy: take away my sin.

  O Jesus, if thou wilt not save my soul,
Who may be saved? who is it may be saved?
Who may be made a saint, if I fail here?
Show me the man hath suffer'd more than I.
For did not all thy martyrs die one death?
For either they were stoned, or crucified,   50
Or burn'd in fire, or boil'd in oil, or sawn
In twain beneath the ribs; but I die here

64

To-day, and whole years long, a life of death.
Bear witness, if I could have found a way
(And heedfully I sifted all my thought)
More slowly-painful to subdue this home
Of sin, my flesh, which I despise and hate,
I had not stinted practice, O my God.

For not alone this pillar-punishment,
Not this alone I bore: but while I lived   60
In the white convent down the valley there,
For many weeks about my loins I wore
The rope that haled the buckets from the well,
Twisted as tight as I could knot the noose;
And spake not of it to a single soul,
Until the ulcer, eating thro' my skin,
Betray'd my secret penance, so that all
My brethren marvell'd greatly. More than this
I bore, whereof, O God, thou knowest all.

Three winters, that my soul might grow to thee,   70
I lived up there on yonder mountain side.
My right leg chain'd into the crag, I lay
Pent in a roofless close of ragged stones;
Inswathed sometimes in wandering mist, and twice
Black'd with thy branding thunder, and sometimes
Sucking the damps for drink, and eating not,
Except the spare chance-gift of those that came
To touch my body and be heal'd, and live:
And they say then that I work'd miracles,
Whereof my fame is loud amongst mankind,   80
Cured lameness, palsies, cancers. Thou, O God,
Knowest alone whether this was or no.
Have mercy, mercy! cover all my sin.

Then, that I might be more alone with thee,
Three years I lived upon a pillar, high
Six cubits, and three years on one of twelve;
And twice three years I crouch'd on one that rose
Twenty by measure; last of all, I grew

Twice ten long weary weary years to this,
That numbers forty cubits from the soil.   90

   I think that I have borne as much as this –
Or else I dream – and for so long a time,
If I may measure time by yon slow light,
And this high dial, which my sorrow crowns –
So much – even so.
              And yet I know not well,
For that the evil ones come here, and say,
'Fall down, O Simeon: thou hast suffer'd long
For ages and for ages!' then they prate
Of penances I cannot have gone thro',
Perplexing me with lies; and oft I fall,   100
Maybe for months, in such blind lethargies
That Heaven, and Earth, and Time are choked.
                   But yet
Bethink thee, Lord, while thou and all the saints
Enjoy themselves in heaven, and men on earth
House in the shade of comfortable roofs,
Sit with their wives by fires, eat wholesome food,
And wear warm clothes, and even beasts have stalls,
I, 'tween the spring and downfall of the light,
Bow down one thousand and two hundred times,
To Christ, the Virgin Mother, and the saints;   110
Or in the night, after a little sleep,
I wake: the chill stars sparkle; I am wet
With drenching dews, or stiff with crackling frost.
I wear an undress'd goatskin on my back;
A grazing iron collar grinds my neck;
And in my weak, lean arms I lift the cross,
And strive and wrestle with thee till I die:
O mercy, mercy! wash away my sin.

   O Lord, thou knowest what a man I am;
A sinful man, conceived and born in sin: 120
'Tis their own doing; this is none of mine;
Lay it not to me. Am I to blame for this,
That here come those that worship me? Ha! ha!

They think that I am somewhat. What am I?
The silly people take me for a saint,
And bring me offerings of fruit and flowers:
And I, in truth (thou wilt bear witness here)
Have all in all endured as much, and more
Than many just and holy men, whose names
Are register'd and calendar'd for saints.   130

Good people, you do ill to kneel to me.
What is it I can have done to merit this?
I am a sinner viler than you all.
It may be I have wrought some miracles,
And cured some halt and maim'd; but what of that?
It may be, no one, even among the saints,
May match his pains with mine; but what of that?
Yet do not rise; for you may look on me,
And in your looking you may kneel to God.
Speak! is there any of you halt or maim'd?   140
I think you know I have some power with Heaven
From my long penance: let him speak his wish.

Yes, I can heal him. Power goes forth from me.
They say that they are heal'd. Ah, hark! they shout
'St Simeon Stylites.' Why, if so,
God reaps a harvest in me. O my soul,
God reaps a harvest in thee. If this be,
Can I work miracles and not be saved?
This is not told of any. They were saints.
It cannot be but that I shall be saved;   150
Yea, crown'd a saint. They shout, 'Behold a saint!'
And lower voices saint me from above.
Courage, St. Simeon! This dull chrysalis
Cracks into shining wings, and hope ere death
Spreads more and more and more, that God hath now
Sponged and made blank of crimeful record all
My mortal archives.
                    O my sons, my sons,
I, Simeon of the pillar, by surname
Stylites, among men; I, Simeon,

67

The watcher on the column till the end;   160
I, Simeon, whose brain the sunshine bakes;
I, whose bald brows in silent hours become
Unnaturally hoar with rime, do now
From my high nest of penance here proclaim
That Pontius and Iscariot by my side
Show'd like fair seraphs. On the coals I lay,
A vessel full of sin: all hell beneath
Made me boil over. Devils pluck'd my sleeve,
Abaddon and Asmodeus caught at me.
I smote them with the cross; they swarm'd again.   170
In bed like monstrous apes they crush'd my chest:
They flapp'd my light out as I read: I saw
Their faces grow between me and my book;
With colt-like whinny and with hoggish whine
They burst my prayer. Yet this way was left,
And by this way I 'scaped them. Mortify
Your flesh, like me, with scourges and with thorns;
Smite, shrink not, spare not. If it may be, fast
Whole Lents, and pray. I hardly, with slow steps,
With slow, faint steps, and much exceeding pain,   180
Have scrambled past those pits of fire, that still
Sing in mine ears. But yield not me the praise:
God only thro' his bounty hath thought fit,
Among the powers and princes of this world,
To make me an example to mankind,
Which few can reach to. Yet I do not say
But that a time may come – yea, even now,
Now, now, his footsteps smite the threshold stairs
Of life – I say, that time is at the doors
When you may worship me without reproach;   190
For I will leave my relics in your land,
And you may carve a shrine about my dust,
And burn a fragrant lamp before my bones,
When I am gather'd to the glorious saints.

    While I spake then, a sting of shrewdest pain
Ran shrivelling thro' me, and a cloudlike change,
In passing, with a grosser film made thick

These heavy, horny eyes. The end! the end!
Surely the end! What's here? a shape, a shade,
A flash of light. Is that the angel there   200
That holds a crown? Come, blessed brother, come.
I know thy glittering face. I waited long;
My brows are ready. What! deny it now?
Nay, draw, draw, draw nigh. So I clutch it. Christ!
'Tis gone: 'tis here again; the crown! the crown!
So now 'tis fitted on and grows to me,
And from it melt the dews of Paradise,
Sweet! sweet! spikenard, and balm, and frankincense.
Ah! let me not be fool'd, sweet saints: I trust
That I am whole, and clean, and meet for Heaven.   210

    Speak, if there be a priest, a man of God,
Among you there, and let him presently
Approach, and lean a ladder on the shaft,
And climbing up into my airy home,
Deliver me the blessed sacrament;
For by the warning of the Holy Ghost,
I prophesy that I shall die to-night,
A quarter before twelve.
                          But thou, O Lord,
Aid all this foolish people; let them take
Example, pattern: lead them to thy light.   220

ULYSSES

It little profits that an idle king,
By this still hearth, among these barren crags,
Match'd with an aged wife, I mete and dole
Unequal laws unto a savage race,
That hoard, and sleep, and feed, and know not me.

I cannot rest from travel: I will drink
Life to the lees: all times I have enjoy'd
Greatly, have suffer'd greatly, both with those
That loved me, and alone; on shore, and when
Thro' scudding drifts the rainy Hyades   10

69

Vext the dim sea: I am become a name;
For always roaming with a hungry heart
Much have I seen and known; cities of men
And manners, climates, councils, governments,
Myself not least, but honour'd of them all;
And drunk delight of battle with my peers,
Far on the ringing plains of windy Troy.
I am a part of all that I have met;
Yet all experience is an arch wherethro'
Gleams that untravell'd world, whose margin fades   20
For ever and for ever when I move.
How dull it is to pause, to make an end,
To rust unburnish'd, not to shine in use!
As tho' to breathe were life. Life piled on life
Were all too little, and of one to me
Little remains: but every hour is saved
From that eternal silence, something more,
A bringer of new things; and vile it were
For some three suns to store and hoard myself,
And this gray spirit yearning in desire   30
To follow knowledge like a sinking star,
Beyond the utmost bound of human thought.

    This is my son, mine own Telemachus,
To whom I leave the sceptre and the isle —
Well-loved of me, discerning to fulfil
This labour, by slow prudence to make mild
A rugged people, and thro' soft degrees
Subdue them to the useful and the good.
Most blameless is he, centred in the sphere
Of common duties, decent not to fail   40
In offices of tenderness, and pay
Meet adoration to my household gods,
When I am gone. He works his work, I mine.

    There lies the port; the vessel puffs her sail:
There gloom the dark broad seas. My mariners,
Souls that have toil'd, and wrought, and thought with me —
That ever with a frolic welcome took

The thunder and the sunshine, and opposed
Free hearts, free foreheads – you and I are old;
Old age hath yet his honour and his toil;   50
Death closes all: but something ere the end,
Some work of noble note, may yet be done,
Not unbecoming men that strove with Gods.
The lights begin to twinkle from the rocks:
The long day wanes: the slow moon climbs: the deep
Moans round with many voices. Come, my friends,
'Tis not too late to seek a newer world.
Push off, and sitting well in order smite
The sounding furrows; for my purpose holds
To sail beyond the sunset, and the baths   60
Of all the western stars, until I die.
It may be that the gulfs will wash us down:
It may be we shall touch the Happy Isles,
And see the great Achilles, whom we knew.
Tho' much is taken, much abides; and tho'
We are not now that strength which in old days
Moved earth and heaven; that which we are, we are;
One equal temper of heroic hearts,
Made weak by time and fate, but strong in will
To strive, to seek, to find, and not to yield.   70

TIRESIAS

I wish I were as in the years of old,
While yet the blessed daylight made itself
Ruddy through both the roofs of sight, and woke
These eyes, now dull, but then so keen to seek
The meanings ambushed under all they saw,
The flight of birds, the flame of sacrifice,
What omens may foreshadow fate to man
And woman, and the secret of the Gods.

    My son, the Gods, despite of human prayer,
Are slower to forgive than human kings.   10
The great God, Arês, burns in anger still
Against the guiltless heirs of him from Tyre,
Our Cadmus, out of whom thou art, who found

Beside the springs of Dircê, smote, and stilled
Through all its folds the multitudinous beast,
The dragon, which our trembling fathers called
The God's own son.

             A tale, that told to me,
When but thine age, by age as winter-white
As mine is now, amazed, but made me yearn
For larger glimpses of that more than man   20
Which rolls the heavens, and lifts, and lays the deep,
Yet loves and hates with mortal hates and loves,
And moves unseen among the ways of men.

    Then, in my wanderings all the lands that lie
Subjected to the Heliconian ridge
Have heard this footstep fall, although my wont
Was more to scale the highest of the heights
With some strange hope to see the nearer God.

    One naked peak – the sister of the sun
Would climb from out the dark, and linger there   30
To silver all the valleys with her shafts –
There once, but long ago, five-fold thy term
Of years, I lay; the winds were dead for heat;
The noonday crag made the hand burn; and sick
For shadow – not one bush was near – I rose
Following a torrent till its myriad falls
Found silence in the hollows underneath.

    There in a secret olive-glade I saw
Pallas Athene climbing from the bath
In anger; yet one glittering foot disturbed   40
The lucid well; one snowy knee was prest
Against the margin flowers; a dreadful light
Came from her golden hair; her golden helm
And all her golden armour on the grass,
And from her virgin breast, and virgin eyes
Remaining fixt on mine, till mine grew dark
For ever, and I heard a voice that said
'Henceforth be blind, for thou hast seen too much,
And speak the truth that no man may believe.'

    Son, in the hidden world of sight, that lives   50
Behind this darkness, I behold her still,

Beyond all work of those who carve the stone,
Beyond all dreams of Godlike womanhood,
Ineffable beauty, out of whom, at a glance,
And as it were, perforce, upon me flashed
The power of prophesying – but to me
No power – so chained and coupled with the curse
Of blindness and their unbelief, who heard
And heard not, when I spake of famine, plague,
Shrine-shattering earthquake, fire, flood, thunderbolt,   60
And angers of the Gods for evil done
And expiation lacked – no power on Fate,
Theirs, or mine own! for when the crowd would roar
For blood, for war, whose issue was their doom,
To cast wise words among the multitude
Was flinging fruit to lions; nor, in hours
Of civil outbreak, when I knew the twain
Would each waste each, and bring on both the yoke
Of stronger states, was mine the voice to curb
The madness of our cities and their kings.   70

Who ever turned upon his heel to hear
My warning that the tyranny of one
Was prelude to the tyranny of all?
My counsel that the tyranny of all
Led backward to the tyranny of one?

This power hath worked no good to aught that lives,
And these blind hands were useless in their wars.
O therefore that the unfulfilled desire,
The grief for ever born from griefs to be,
The boundless yearning of the Prophet's heart –   80
Could *that* stand forth, and like a statue, reared
To some great citizen, win all praise from all
Who past it, saying, 'That was he!'
                                        In vain!
Virtue must shape itself in deed, and those
Whom weakness or necessity have cramped
Within themselves, immerging, each, his urn
In his own well, draw solace as he may.

Menœceus, thou hast eyes, and I can hear
Too plainly what full tides of onset sap

73

Our seven high gates, and what a weight of war   90
Rides on those ringing axles! jingle of bits,
Shouts, arrows, tramp of the hornfooted horse
That grind the glebe to powder! Stony showers
Of that ear-stunning hail of Arês crash
Along the sounding walls. Above, below,
Shock after shock, the song-built towers and gates
Reel, bruised and butted with the shuddering
War-thunder of iron rams; and from within
The city comes a murmur void of joy,
Lest she be taken captive – maidens, wives,   100
And mothers with their babblers of the dawn,
And oldest age in shadow from the night,
Falling about their shrines before their Gods,
And wailing 'Save us.'
               And they wail to thee!
These eyeless eyes, that cannot see thine own,
See this, that only in thy virtue lies
The saving of our Thebes; for, yesternight,
To me, the great God Arês, whose one bliss
Is war, and human sacrifice – himself
Blood-red from battle, spear and helmet tipt   110
With stormy light as on a mast at sea,
Stood out before a darkness, crying 'Thebes,
Thy Thebes shall fall and perish, for I loathe
The seed of Cadmus – yet if one of these
By his own hand – if one of these –'
                     My son,
No sound is breathed so potent to coerce,
And to conciliate, as their names who dare
For that sweet mother land which gave them birth
Nobly to do, nobly to die. Their names,
Graven on memorial columns, are a song   120
Heard in the future; few, but more than wall
And rampart, their examples reach a hand
Far through all years, and everywhere they meet
And kindle generous purpose, and the strength
To mould it into action pure as theirs.
  Fairer thy fate than mine, if life's best end

74

Be to end well! and thou refusing this,
Unvenerable will thy memory be
While men shall move the lips: but if thou dare —
Thou, one of these, the race of Cadmus — then   130
No stone is fitted in yon marble girth
Whose echo shall not tongue thy glorious doom,
Nor in this pavement but shall ring thy name
To every hoof that clangs it, and the springs
Of Dircê laving yonder battle-plain,
Heard from the roofs by night, will murmur thee
To thine own Thebes, while Thebes through thee shall stand
Firm-based with all her Gods.
                                        The Dragon's cave
Half hid, they tell me, now in flowing vines —
Where once he dwelt and whence he rolled himself   140
At dead of night — thou knowest, and that smooth rock
Before it, altar-fashioned, where of late
The woman-breasted Sphinx, with wings drawn back,
Folded her lion paws, and looked to Thebes.
There blanch the bones of whom she slew, and these
Mixt with her own, because the fierce beast found
A wiser than herself, and dashed herself
Dead in her rage: but thou art wise enough,
Though young, to love thy wiser, blunt the curse
Of Pallas, hear, and though I speak the truth   150
Believe I speak it, let thine own hand strike
Thy youthful pulses into rest and quench
The red God's anger, fearing not to plunge
Thy torch of life in darkness, rather — thou
Rejoicing that the sun, the moon, the stars
Send no such light upon the ways of men
As one great deed.
                        Thither, my son, and there
Thou, that hast never known the embrace of love,
Offer thy maiden life.
                        This useless hand!
I felt one warm tear fall upon it. Gone!   160
He will achieve his greatness.
                        But for me,

75

I would that I were gathered to my rest,
And mingled with the famous kings of old,
On whom about their ocean-islets flash
The faces of the Gods – the wise man's word,
Here trampled by the populace underfoot,
There crowned with worship – and these eyes will find
The men I knew, and watch the chariot whirl
About the goal again, and hunters race
The shadowy lion, and the warrior-kings,   170
In height and prowess more than human, strive
Again for glory, while the golden lyre
Is ever sounding in heroic ears
Heroic hymns, and every way the vales
Wind, clouded with the grateful incense-fume
Of those who mix all odour to the Gods
On one far height in one far-shining fire.

BREAK, BREAK, BREAK

Break, break, break,
  On thy cold gray stones, O Sea!
And I would that my tongue could utter
  The thoughts that arise in me.

O well for the fisherman's boy,
  That he shouts with his sister at play!
O well for the sailor lad,
  That he sings in his boat on the bay!

And the stately ships go on
  To their haven under the hill;
But O for the touch of a vanish'd hand,
  And the sound of a voice that is still!

Break, break, break,
  At the foot of thy crags, O Sea!
But the tender grace of a day that is dead
  Will never come back to me.

THE EPIC

At Francis Allen's on the Christmas-eve, –
The game of forfeits done – the girls all kiss'd
Beneath the sacred bush and past away –
The parson Holmes, the poet Everard Hall,
The host, and I sat round the wassail-bowl,
Then half-way ebb'd: and there we held a talk,
How all the old honour had from Christmas gone,
Or gone, or dwindled down to some odd games
In some odd nooks like this; till I, tired out
With cutting eights that day upon the pond,   10
Where, three times slipping from the outer edge,
I bump'd the ice into three several stars,
Fell in a doze; and half-awake I heard
The parson taking wide and wider sweeps,
Now harping on the church-commissioners,
Now hawking at Geology and schism;
Until I woke, and found him settled down
Upon the general decay of faith
Right thro' the world, 'at home was little left,
And none abroad: there was no anchor, none,   20
To hold by.' Francis, laughing, clapt his hand
On Everard's shoulder, with 'I hold by him.'
'And I,' quoth Everard, 'by the wassail-bowl.'
'Why yes,' I said, 'we knew your gift that way
At college: but another which you had,
I mean of verse (for so we held it then),
What came of that?' 'You know,' said Frank, 'he burnt
His epic, his King Arthur, some twelve books' –
And then to me demanding why? 'Oh, sir,
He thought that nothing new was said, or else   30
Something so said 'twas nothing – that a truth
Looks freshest in the fashion of the day:
God knows: he has a mint of reasons: ask.
It pleased *me* well enough.' 'Nay, nay,' said Hall,
'Why take the style of those heroic times?
For nature brings not back the Mastodon,
Nor we those times; and why should any man

Remodel models? these twelve books of mine
Were faint Homeric echoes, nothing-worth,
Mere chaff and draff, much better burnt.' 'But I,'   40
Said Francis, 'pick'd the eleventh from this hearth
And have it: keep a thing, its use will come.
I hoard it as a sugar-plum for Holmes.'
He laugh'd, and I, tho' sleepy, like a horse
That hears the corn-bin open, prick'd my ears;
For I remember'd Everard's college fame
When we were Freshmen: then at my request
He brought it; and the poet little urged,
But with some prelude of disparagement,
Read, mouthing out his hollow oes and aes,   50
Deep-chested music, and to this result.

MORTE D'ARTHUR

So all day long the noise of battle roll'd
Among the mountains by the winter sea;
Until King Arthur's table, man by man,
Had fallen in Lyonnesse about their Lord,
King Arthur: then, because his would was deep,
The bold Sir Bedivere uplifted him,
Sir Bedivere, the last of all his knights,
And bore him to a chapel nigh the field,
A broken chancel with a broken cross,
That stood on a dark strait of barren land.   10
On one side lay the Ocean, and on one
Lay a great water, and the moon was full.

    Then spake King Arthur to Sir Bedivere:
'The sequel of to-day unsolders all
The goodliest fellowship of famous knights
Whereof this world holds record. Such a sleep
They sleep – the men I loved. I think that we
Shall never more, at any future time,
Delight our souls with talk of knightly deeds,
Walking about the gardens and the halls   20
Of Camelot, as in the days that were.

78

I perish by this people which I made, –
Tho' Merlin sware that I should come again
To rule once more – but let what will be, be,
I am so deeply smitten thro' the helm
That without help I cannot last till morn.
Thou therefore take my brand Excalibur,
Which was my pride: for thou rememberest how
In those old days, one summer noon, an arm
Rose up from out the bosom of the lake,   30
Clothed in white samite, mystic, wonderful,
Holding the sword – and how I row'd across
And took it, and have worn it, like a king:
And, wheresoever I am sung or told
In aftertime, this also shall be known:
But now delay not: take Excalibur,
And fling him far into the middle mere:
Watch what thou seëst, and lightly bring me word.'

    To him replied the bold Sir Bedivere:
'It is not meet, Sir King, to leave thee thus,   40
Aidless, alone, and smitten thro' the helm.
A little thing may harm a wounded man.
Yet I thy hest will all perform at full,
Watch what I see, and lightly bring thee word.'

    So saying, from the ruin'd shrine he stept
And in the moon athwart the place of tombs,
Where lay the mighty bones of ancient men,
Old knights, and over them the sea-wind sang
Shrill, chill, with flakes of foam. He, stepping down
By zig-zag paths, and juts of pointed rock,   50
Came on the shining levels of the lake.

    There drew he forth the brand Excalibur,
And o'er him, drawing it, the winter moon,
Brightening the skirts of a long cloud, ran forth
And sparkled keen with frost against the hilt:
For all the haft twinkled with diamond sparks,
Myriads of topaz-lights, and jacinth-work

Of subtlest jewellery. He gazed so long
That both his eyes were dazzled, as he stood,
This way and that dividing the swift mind,   60
In act to throw: but at the last it seem'd
Better to leave Excalibur conceal'd
There in the many-knotted waterflags,
That whistled stiff and dry about the marge.
So strode he back slow to the wounded King.

    Then spake King Arthur to Sir Bedivere:
'Hast thou perform'd my mission which I gave?
What is it thou hast seen? or what hast heard?'

    And answer made the bold Sir Bedivere:
'I heard the ripple washing in the reeds,   70
And the wild water lapping on the crag.'

    To whom replied King Arthur, faint and pale:
'Thou hast betray'd thy nature and thy name,
Not rendering true answer, as beseem'd
Thy fëalty, nor like a noble knight:
For surer sign had follow'd, either hand,
Or voice, or else a motion of the mere.
This is a shameful thing for men to lie.
Yet now, I charge thee, quickly go again
As thou art lief and dear, and do the thing   80
I bad thee, watch, and lightly bring me word.'

    Then went Sir Bedivere the second time
Across the ridge, and paced beside the mere,
Counting the dewy pebbles, fix'd in thought;
But when he saw the wonder of the hilt,
How curiously and strangely chased, he smote
His palms together, and he cried aloud,

    'And if indeed I cast the brand away,
Surely a precious thing, one worthy note,
Should thus be lost for ever from the earth,   90
Which might have pleased the eyes of many men.

What good should follow this, if this were done?
What harm, undone? deep harm to disobey,
Seeing obedience is the bond of rule.
Were it well to obey then, if a king demand
An act unprofitable, against himself?
The King is sick, and knows not what he does.
What record, or what relic of my lord
Should be to aftertime, but empty breath
And rumours of a doubt? but were this kept,   100
Stored in some treasure-house of mighty kings,
Some one might show it at a joust of arms,
Saying, "King Arthur's sword, Excalibur,
Wrought by the lonely maiden of the Lake.
Nine years she wrought it, sitting in the deeps
Upon the hidden bases of the hills."
So might some old man speak in the aftertime
To all the people, winning reverence.
But now much honour and much fame were lost.'

So spake he, clouded with his own conceit,   110
And hid Excalibur the second time,
And so strode back slow to the wounded King.

Then spoke King Arthur, breathing heavily:
'What is it thou hast seen? or what hast heard?'

And answer made the bold Sir Bedivere:
'I heard the water lapping on the crag,
And the long ripple washing in the reeds.'

To whom replied King Arthur, much in wrath:
'Ah, miserable and unkind, untrue,
Unknightly, traitor-hearted! Woe is me!   120
Authority forgets a dying king,
Laid widow'd of the power in his eye
That bow'd the will. I see thee what thou art,
For thou, the latest-left of all my knights,
In whom should meet the offices of all,
Thou wouldst betray me for the precious hilt;

Either from lust of gold, or like a girl
Valuing the giddy pleasure of the eyes.
Yet, for a man may fail in duty twice,
And the third time may prosper, get thee hence: 130
But, if thou spare to fling Excalibur,
I will arise and slay thee with my hands.'

Then quickly rose Sir Bedivere, and ran,
And, leaping down the ridges lightly, plunged
Among the bulrush-beds, and clutch'd the sword,
And strongly wheel'd and threw it. The great brand
Made lightnings in the splendour of the moon,
And flashing round and round, and whirl'd in an arch,
Shot like a streamer of the northern morn,
Seen where the moving isles of winter shock   140
By night, with noises of the northern sea.
So flash'd and fell the brand Excalibur:
But ere he dipt the surface, rose an arm
Clothed in white samite, mystic, wonderful,
And caught him by the hilt, and brandish'd him
Three times, and drew him under in the mere.
And lightly went the other to the King.

Then spoke King Arthur, drawing thicker breath:
'Now see I by thine eyes that this is done.
Speak out: what is it thou hast heard, or seen?'   150

And answer made the bold Sir Bedivere:
'Sir King, I closed mine eyelids, lest the gems
Should blind my purpose, for I never saw,
Nor shall see, here or elsewhere, till I die,
Not tho' I live three lives of mortal men,
So great a miracle as yonder hilt.
Then with both hands I flung him, wheeling him;
But when I look'd again, behold an arm,
Clothed in white samite, mystic, wonderful,
That caught him by the hilt, and brandish'd him   160
Three times, and drew him under in the mere.'

And answer made King Arthur, breathing hard:
'My end draws nigh; 'tis time that I were gone.
Make broad thy shoulders to receive my weight,
And bear me to the margin; yet I fear
My wound hath taken cold, and I shall die.'

So saying, from the pavement he half rose,
Slowly, with pain, reclining on his arm,
And looking wistfully with wide blue eyes
As in a picture. Him Sir Bedivere   170
Remorsefully regarded thro' his tears,
And would have spoken, but he found not words,
Then took with care, and kneeling on one knee,
O'er both his shoulders drew the languid hands,
And rising bore him thro' the place of tombs.

But, as he walk'd, King Arthur panted hard,
Like one that feels a nightmare on his bed
When all the house is mute. So sigh'd the King,
Muttering and murmuring at his ear, 'Quick, quick!
I fear it is too late, and I shall die.'   180
But the other swiftly strode from ridge to ridge,
Clothed with his breath, and looking, as he walk'd,
Larger than human on the frozen hills.
He heard the deep behind him, and a cry
Before. His own thought drove him, like a goad.
Dry clash'd his harness in the icy caves
And barren chasms, and all to left and right
The bare black cliff clang'd round him, as he based
His feet on juts of slippery crag that rang
Sharp-smitten with the dint of armed heels —   190
And on a sudden, lo! the level lake,
And the long glories of the winter moon.

Then saw they how there hove a dusky barge,
Dark as a funeral scarf from stem to stern,
Beneath them; and descending they were ware
That all the decks were dense with stately forms
Black-stoled, black-hooded, like a dream — by these

Three Queens with crowns of gold – and from them rose
A cry that shiver'd to the tingling stars,
And, as it were one voice, an agony   200
Of lamentation, like a wind, that shrills
All night in a waste land, where no one comes,
Or hath come, since the making of the world.

    Then murmur'd Arthur, 'Place me in the barge,'
And to the barge they came. There those three Queens
Put forth their hands, and took the King, and wept.
But she, that rose the tallest of them all
And fairest, laid his head upon her lap,
And loosed the shatter'd casque, and chafed his hands,
And call'd him by his name, complaining loud,   210
And dropping bitter tears against his brow
Striped with dark blood: for all his face was white
And colourless, and like the wither'd moon
Smote by the fresh beam of the springing east;
And all his greaves and cuisses dash'd with drops
Of onset; and the light and lustrous curls –
That made his forehead like a rising sun
High from the daïs-throne – were parch'd with dust;
Or, clotted into points and hanging loose,
Mix'd with the knightly growth that fringed his lips.   220
So like a shatter'd column lay the King;
Not like that Arthur who, with lance in rest,
From spur to plume a star of tournament,
Shot thro' the lists at Camelot, and charged
Before the eyes of ladies and of kings.

    Then loudly cried the bold Sir Bedivere,
'Ah! my Lord Arthur, whither shall I go?
Where shall I hide my forehead and my eyes?
For now I see the true old times are dead,
When every morning brought a noble chance,
And every chance brought out a noble knight.
Such times have been not since the light that led
The holy Elders with the gift of myrrh.
But now the whole ROUND TABLE is dissolved

Which was an image of the mighty world;
And I, the last, go forth companionless,
And the days darken round me, and the years,
Among new men, strange faces, other minds.'

And slowly answered Arthur from the barge:
'The old order changeth, yielding place to new,
And God fulfils Himself in many ways,   240
Lest one good custom should corrupt the world.
Comfort thyself: what comfort is in me?
I have lived my life, and that which I have done
May He within Himself make pure! but thou,
If thou shouldst never see my face again,
Pray for my soul. More things are wrought by prayer
Than this world dreams of. Wherefore, let thy voice
Rise like a fountain for me night and day.
For what are men better than sheep or goats   250
That nourish a blind life within the brain,
If, knowing God, they lift not hands of prayer
Both for themselves and those who call them friend?
For so the whole round earth is every way
Bound by gold chains about the feet of God.
But now farewell. I am going a long way
With these thou seëst – if indeed I go –
(For all my mind is clouded with a doubt)
To the island-valley of Avilion;
Where falls not hail, or rain, or any snow,   260
Nor ever wind blows loudly; but it lies
Deep-meadow'd, happy, fair with orchard-lawns
And bowery hollows crown'd with summer sea,
Where I will heal me of my grievous wound.'

So said he, and the barge with oar and sail
Moved from the brink, like some full-breasted swan
That, fluting a wild carol ere her death,
Ruffles her pure cold plume, and takes the flood
With swarthy webs. Long stood Sir Bedivere
Revolving many memories, till the hull   270
Look'd one black dot against the verge of dawn,

And on the mere the wailing died away.

Here ended Hall, and our last light, that long
Had wink'd and threaten'd darkness, flared and fell:
At which the Parson, sent to sleep with sound,
And waked with silence, grunted 'Good!' but we
Sat rapt: it was the tone with which he read –
Perhaps some modern touches here and there
Redeem'd it from the charge of nothingness –
Or else we loved the man, and prized his work;   280
I know not: but we sitting, as I said,
The cock crew loud; as at that time of year
The lusty bird takes every hour for dawn:
Then Francis, muttering, like a man ill-used,
'There now – that's nothing!' drew a little back,
And drove his heel into the smoulder'd log,
That sent a blast of sparkles up the flue:
And so to bed; where yet in sleep I seem'd
To sail with Arthur under looming shores,
Point after point; till on to dawn, when dreams   290
Begin to feel the truth and stir of day,
To me, methought, who waited with a crowd,
There came a bark that, blowing forward, bore
King Arthur, like a modern gentleman
Of stateliest port; and all the people cried,
'Arthur is come again: he cannot die.'
Then those that stood upon the hills behind
Repeated – 'Come again, and thrice as fair;'
And, further inland, voices echo'd – 'Come
With all good things, and war shall be no more.'   300
At this a hundred bells began to peal,
That with the sound I woke, and heard indeed
The clear church-bells ring in the Christmas-morn.

WALKING TO THE MAIL

John I'm glad I walk'd. How fresh the meadows look
Above the river, and, but a month ago,
The whole hill-side was redder than a fox.
Is yon plantation where this byway joins
The turnpike?
   James   Yes.
   John   And when does this come by?
   James The mail? At one o'clock.
   John   What is it now?
   James A quarter to.
   John   Whose house is that I see?
No, not the County Member's with the vane:
Up higher with the yew-tree by it, and half
A score of gables.
   James   That? Sir Edward Head's: 10
But he's abroad: the place is to be sold.
   John Oh, his. He was not broken.
   James   No, sir, he,
Vex'd with a morbid devil in his blood
That veil'd the world with jaundice, hid his face
From all men, and commercing with himself,
He lost the sense that handles daily life –
That keeps us all in order more or less –
And sick of home went overseas for change.
   John And whither?
   James   Nay, who knows? he's here and there.
But let him go; his devil goes with him,   20
As well as with his tenant, Jocky Dawes.
   John What's that?
   James   You saw the man – on Monday, was it? –
There by the humpback'd willow; half stands up
And bristles; half has fall'n and made a bridge;
And there he caught the younker tickling trout –
Caught *in flagrante* – what's the Latin word? –
Delicto: but his house, for so they say,
Was haunted with a jolly ghost, that shook
The curtains, whined in lobbies, tapt at doors,   30

And rummaged like a rat: no servant stay'd:
The farmer vext packs up his beds and chairs,
And all his household stuff; and with his boy
Betwixt his knees, his wife upon the tilt,
Sets out, and meets a friend who hails him, 'What!
You're flitting!' 'Yes, we're flitting,' says the ghost
(For they had pack'd the thing among the beds,)
'Oh well,' says he, 'you flitting with us too –
Jack, turn the horses' heads and home again.'
   John He left *his* wife behind; for so I heard.
   James He left her, yes. I met my lady once: 40
A woman like a butt, and harsh as crabs.
   John Oh yet but I remember, ten years back –
'Tis now at least ten years – and then she was –
You could not light upon a sweeter thing:
A body slight and round, and like a pear
In growing, modest eyes, a hand, a foot
Lessening in perfect cadence, and a skin
As clean and white as privet when it flowers.
   James Ay, ay, the blossom fades, and they that loved
At first like dove and dove were cat and dog.   50
She was the daughter of a cottager,
Out of her sphere. What betwixt shame and pride,
New things and old, himself and her, she sour'd
To what she is: a nature never kind!
Like men, like manners: like breeds like, they say:
Kind nature is the best: those manners next
That fit us like a nature second-hand;
Which are indeed the manners of the great.
   John But I had heard it was this bill that past,
And fear of change at home, that drove him hence.   60
   James That was the last drop in the cup of gall.
I once was near him, when his bailiff brought
A Chartist pike. You should have seen him wince
As from a venomous thing: he thought himself
A mark for all, and shudder'd, lest a cry
Should break his sleep by night, and his nice eyes
Should see the raw mechanic's bloody thumbs
Sweat on his blazon'd chairs; but, sir, you know

That these two parties still divide the world –
Of those that want, and those that have: and still   70
The same old sore breaks out from age to age
With much the same result. Now I myself,
A Tory to the quick, was as a boy
Destructive, when I had not what I would.
I was at school – a college in the South:
There lived a flayflint near; we stole his fruit,
His hens, his eggs; but there was law for *us*;
We paid in person. He had a sow, sir. She,
With meditative grunts of much content,
Lay great with pig, wallowing in sun and mud.   80
By night we dragg'd her to the college tower
From her warm bed, and up the corkscrew stair
With hand and rope we haled the groaning sow,
And on the leads we kept her till she pigg'd.
Large range of prospect had the mother sow,
And but for daily loss of one she loved
As one by one we took them – but for this –
As never sow was higher in this world –
Might have been happy: but what lot is pure?
We took them all, till she was left alone   90
Upon her tower, the Niobe of swine,
And so return'd unfarrow'd to her sty.

   John They found you out?
   James   Not they.
   John   Well – after all –
What know we of the secret of a man?
His nerves were wrong. What ails us, who are sound,
That we should mimic this raw fool the world,
Which charts us all in its coarse blacks or whites,
As ruthless as a baby with a worm,
As cruel as a schoolboy ere he grows
To Pity – more from ignorance than will.   100

   But put your best foot forward, or I fear
That we shall miss the mail: and here it comes
With five at top: as quaint a four-in-hand
As you shall see – three pyebalds and a roan.

89

LOCKSLEY HALL

Comrades, leave me here a little, while as yet 'tis early morn:
Leave me here, and when you want me, sound upon the bugle-
    horn.

'Tis the place, and all around it, as of old, the curlews call,
Dreary gleams about the moorland flying over Locksley Hall;

Locksley Hall, that in the distance overlooks the sandy tracts,
And the hollow ocean-ridges roaring into cataracts.

Many a night from yonder ivied casement, ere I went to rest,
Did I look on great Orion sloping slowly to the West.

Many a night I saw the Pleiads, rising thro' the mellow
    shade,
Glitter like a swarm of fire-flies tangled in a silver braid.   10

Here about the beach I wander'd, nourishing a youth sublime
With the fairy tales of science, and the long result of Time;

When the centuries behind me like a fruitful land reposed;
When I clung to all the present for the promise that it closed:

When I dipt into the future far as human eye could see;
Saw the Vision of the world, and all the wonder that would
    be.——

In the Spring a fuller crimson comes upon the robin's breast;
In the Spring the wanton lapwing gets himself another crest;

In the Spring a livelier iris changes on the burnish'd dove;
In the Spring a young man's fancy lightly turns to thoughts
    of love.   20

Then her cheek was pale and thinner than should be for one so
    young,
And her eyes on all my motions with a mute observance hung.

And I said, 'My cousin Amy, speak, and speak the truth to me,
Trust me, cousin, all the current of my being sets to thee.'

On her pallid cheek and forehead came a colour and a light,
As I have seen the rosy red flushing in the northern night.

And she turn'd – her bosom shaken with a sudden storm of
    sighs –
All the spirit deeply dawning in the dark of hazel eyes –

Saying, 'I have hid my feelings, fearing they should do me
    wrong;'
Saying, 'Dost thou love me, cousin?' weeping, 'I have loved
    thee long.'   30

Love took up the glass of Time, and turn'd it in his glowing
    hands;
Every moment, lightly shaken, ran itself in golden sands.

Love took up the harp of Life, and smote on all the chords with
    might;
Smote the chord of Self, that, trembling, pass'd in music out of
    sight.

Many a morning on the moorland did we hear the copses ring,
And her whisper throng'd my pulses with the fulness of the
    Spring.

Many an evening by the waters did we watch the stately ships,
And our spirits rush'd together at the touching of the lips.

O my cousin, shallow-hearted! O my Amy, mine no more!
O the dreary, dreary moorland! O the barren, barren shore!   40

Falser than all fancy fathoms, falser than all songs have sung,
Puppet to a father's threat, and servile to a shrewish tongue!

Is it well to wish thee happy? – having known me – to decline
On a range of lower feelings and a narrower heart than mine!

Yet it shall be: thou shalt lower to his level day by day,
What is fine within thee growing coarse to sympathize with clay.

As the husband is, the wife is: thou art mated with a clown,
And the grossness of his nature will have weight to drag thee
    down.

He will hold thee, when his passion shall have spent its novel
    force,
Something better than his dog, a little dearer than his horse.   50

What is this? his eyes are heavy: think not they are glazed
    with wine.
Go to him: it is thy duty: kiss him: take his hand in thine.

It may be my lord is weary, that his brain is overwrought:
Soothe him with thy finer fancies, touch him with thy lighter
    thought.

He will answer to the purpose, easy things to understand –
Better thou wert dead before me, tho' I slew thee with
    my hand!

Better thou and I were lying, hidden from the heart's disgrace,
Roll'd in one another's arms, and silent in a last embrace.

Cursed be the social wants that sin against the strength
    of youth!
Cursed be the social lies that warp us from the living truth!   60

Cursed be the sickly forms that err from honest Nature's
    rule!
Cursed be the gold that gilds the straiten'd forehead of the
    fool!

Well – 'tis well that I should bluster! – Hadst thou less unworthy
    proved –
Would to God – for I had loved thee more than ever wife was
    loved.

Am I mad, that I should cherish that which bears but bitter fruit?
I will pluck it from my bosom, tho' my heart be at the root.

Never, tho' my mortal summers to such length of years should
    come
As the many-winter'd crow that leads the clanging rookery
    home.

Where is comfort? in division of the records of the mind?
Can I part her from herself, and love her, as I knew her,
    kind?   70

I remember one that perish'd: sweetly did she speak and move:
Such a one do I remember, whom to look at was to love.

Can I think of her as dead, and love her for the love she bore?
No – she never loved me truly: love is love for evermore.

Comfort? comfort scorn'd of devils! this is truth the poet sings,
That a sorrow's crown of sorrow is remembering happier things.

Drug thy memories, lest thou learn it, lest thy heart be put to
    proof,
In the dead unhappy night, and when the rain is on the roof.

Like a dog, he hunts in dreams, and thou art staring at the wall,
Where the dying night-lamp flickers, and the shadows rise and
    fall.   80

Then a hand shall pass before thee, pointing to his drunken sleep,
To thy widow'd marriage-pillows, to the tears that thou wilt
    weep.

Thou shalt hear the 'Never, never,' whisper'd by the phantom
    years,
And a song from out the distance in the ringing of thine ears;

And an eye shall vex thee, looking ancient kindness on thy pain.
Turn thee, turn thee on thy pillow: get thee to thy rest again.

Nay, but Nature brings thee solace; for a tender voice will cry.
'Tis a purer life than thine; a lip to drain thy trouble dry.

Baby lips will laugh me down: my latest rival brings thee rest.
Baby fingers, waxen touches, press me from the mother's
    breast.   90

O, the child too clothes the father with a dearness not his due.
Half is thine and half is his: it will be worthy of the two.

O, I see thee old and formal, fitted to thy petty part,
With a little hoard of maxims preaching down a daughter's
    heart.

'They were dangerous guides the feelings – she herself was not
    exempt –
Truly, she herself had suffer'd' – Perish in thy self-contempt!

Overlive it – lower yet – be happy! wherefore should I care?
I myself must mix with action, lest I wither by despair.

What is that which I should turn to, lighting upon days like
    these?
Every door is barr'd with gold, and opens but to golden
    keys.   100

Every gate is throng'd with suitors, all the markets overflow.
I have but an angry fancy: what is that which I should do?

I had been content to perish, falling on the foeman's ground,
When the ranks are roll'd in vapour, and the winds are laid with
    sound.

But the jingling of the guinea helps the hurt that Honour feels,
And the nations do but murmur, snarling at each other's heels.

Can I but relive in sadness? I will turn that earlier page.
Hide me from my deep emotion, O thou wondrous
    Mother-Age!

Make me feel the wild pulsation that I felt before the strife,
When I heard my days before me, and the tumult of my life; 110

Yearning for the large excitement that the coming years would
    yield,
Eager-hearted as a boy when first he leaves his father's field,

And at night along the dusky highway near and nearer drawn,
Sees in heaven the light of London flaring like a dreary dawn;

And his spirit leaps within him to be gone before him then,
Underneath the light he looks at, in among the throngs
    of men:

Men, my brothers, men the workers, ever reaping something
    new:
That which they have done but earnest of the things that they
    shall do:

For I dipt into the future, far as human eye could see,
Saw the Vision of the world, and all the wonder that
    would be;   120

Saw the heavens fill with commerce, argosies of magic sails,
Pilots of the purple twilight, dropping down with costly
    bales;

Heard the heavens fill with shouting, and there rain'd a ghastly
    dew
From the nations' airy navies grappling in the central blue;

Far along the world-wide whisper of the south-wind rushing
    warm,
With the standards of the peoples plunging thro' the thunder-
    storm;

Till the war-drum throbb'd no longer, and the battle-flags were
    furl'd
In the Parliament of man, the Federation of the world.

There the common sense of most shall hold a fretful realm in
    awe,
And the kindly earth shall slumber, lapt in universal law.   130

So I triumph'd ere my passion sweeping thro' me left me dry,
Left me with the palsied heart, and left me with the jaundiced
    eye;

Eye, to which all order festers, all things here are out of joint:
Science moves, but slowly slowly, creeping on from point to
        point:

Slowly comes a hungry people, as a lion creeping nigher,
Glares at one that nods and winks behind a slowly-dying fire.

Yet I doubt not thro' the ages one increasing purpose runs,
And the thoughts of men are widen'd with the process of the
    suns.

What is that to him that reaps not harvest of his youthful joys,
Tho' the deep heart of existence beat for ever like a boy's?   140

Knowledge comes, but wisdom lingers, and I linger on the shore,
And the individual withers, and the world is more and more.

Knowledge comes, but wisdom lingers, and he bears a laden
        breast,
Full of sad experience, moving toward the stillness of his rest.

Hark, my merry comrades call me, sounding on the bugle-horn,
They to whom my foolish passion were a target for their scorn:

Shall it not be scorn to me to harp on such a moulder'd string?
I am shamed thro' all my nature to have loved so slight a thing.

Weakness to be wroth with weakness! woman's pleasure, woman's
    pain –
Nature made them blinder motions bounded in a shallower
        brain: 150

Woman is the lesser man, and all thy passions, match'd with mine,
Are as moonlight unto sunlight, and as water unto wine –

Here at least, where nature sickens, nothing. Ah, for some retreat
Deep in yonder shining Orient, where my life began to beat;

Where in wild Mahratta-battle fell my father evil-starr'd; –
I was left a trampled orphan, and a selfish uncle's ward.

Or to burst all links of habit – there to wander far away,
On from island unto island at the gateways of the day.

Larger constellations burning, mellow moons and happy skies,
Breadths of tropic shade and palms in cluster, knots of
     Paradise.   160

Never comes the trader, never floats an European flag,
Slides the bird o'er lustrous woodland, swings the trailer from
     the crag;

Droops the heavy-blossom'd bower, hangs the heavy-fruited
     tree –
Summer isles of Eden lying in dark-purple spheres of sea.

There methinks would be enjoyment more than in this march of
     mind,
In the steamship, in the railway, in the thoughts that shake
     mankind.

There the passions cramp'd no longer shall have scope and
     breathing space;
I will take some savage woman, she shall rear my dusky race.

Iron jointed, supple-sinew'd, they shall dive, and they shall run,
Catch the wild goat by the hair, and hurl their lances in
     the sun;   170

Whistle back the parrot's call, and leap the rainbows of the brooks,
Not with blinded eyesight poring over miserable books –

Fool, again the dream, the fancy! but I *know* my words are wild,
But I count the gray barbarian lower than the Christian child.

I, to herd with narrow foreheads, vacant of our glorious gains,
Like a beast with lower pleasures, like a beast with lower pains!

Mated with a squalid savage – what to me were sun or clime?
I the heir of all the ages, in the foremost files of time –

I that rather held it better men should perish one by one,
Than that earth should stand at gaze like Joshua's moon in
    Ajalon!   180

Not in vain the distance beacons. Forward, forward let us range,
Let the great world spin for ever down the ringing grooves of
    change.

Thro' the shadow of the globe we sweep into the younger day:
Better fifty years of Europe than a cycle of Cathay.

Mother-Age (for mine I knew not) help me as when life begun:
Rift the hills, and roll the waters, flash the lightnings, weigh the
    Sun.

O, I see the crescent promise of my spirit hath not set.
Ancient founts of inspiration well thro' all my fancy yet.

Howsoever these things be, a long farewell to Locksley Hall!
Now for me the woods may wither, now for me the roof-tree
    fall.   190

Comes a vapour from the margin, blackening over heath and holt,
Cramming all the blast before it, in its breast a thunderbolt.

Let it fall on Locksley Hall, with rain or hail, or fire or snow;
For the mighty wind arises, roaring seaward, and I go.

FROM THE PRINCESS

The splendour falls on castle walls
   And snowy summits old in story:
The long light shakes across the lakes,
   And the wild cataract leaps in glory.
Blow, bugle, blow, set the wild echoes flying,
Blow, bugle; answer, echoes, dying, dying, dying.

O hark, O hear! how thin and clear,
   And thinner, clearer, farther going!
O sweet and far from cliff and scar
   The horns of Elfland faintly blowing!   10
Blow, let us hear the purple glens replying:
Blow, bugle; answer, echoes, dying, dying, dying.

O love, they die in yon rich sky,
   They faint on hill or field or river:
Our echoes roll from soul to soul,
   And grow for ever and for ever.
Blow, bugle, blow, set the wild echoes flying,
And answer, echoes, answer, dying, dying, dying.

★   ★   ★

'Tears, idle tears, I know not what they mean,
Tears from the depth of some divine despair
Rise in the heart, and gather to the eyes,
In looking on the happy Autumn-fields,
And thinking of the days that are no more.

'Fresh as the first beam glittering on a sail,
That brings our friends up from the underworld,
Sad as the last which reddens over one
That sinks with all we love below the verge;
So sad, so fresh, the days that are no more.   10

'Ah, sad and strange as in dark summer dawns
The earliest pipe of half-awakened birds
To dying ears, when unto dying eyes

The casement slowly grows a glimmering square;
So sad, so strange, the days that are no more.

    'Dear as remembered kisses after death,
And sweet as those by hopeless fancy feigned
On lips that are for others; deep as love,
Deep as first love, and wild with all regret;
O Death in Life, the days that are no more.'   20

★ ★ ★

    'Now sleeps the crimson petal, now the white;
Nor waves the cypress in the palace walk;
Nor winks the gold fin in the porphyry font:
The fire-fly wakens: waken thou with me.

    Now droops the milkwhite peacock like a ghost,
And like a ghost she glimmers on to me.

    Now lies the Earth all Danaë to the stars,
And all thy heart lies open unto me.

    Now slides the silent meteor on, and leaves
A shining furrow, as thy thoughts in me.   10

    Now folds the lily all her sweetness up,
And slips into the bosom of the lake:
So fold thyself, my dearest, thou, and slip
Into my bosom and be lost in me.'

From IN MEMORIAM A.H.H.

OBIIT MDCCCXXXIII

[Prologue]

Strong Son of God, immortal Love,
    Whom we, that have not seen thy face,
    By faith, and faith alone, embrace,
Believing where we cannot prove;

100

Thine are those orbs of light and shade;
   Thou madest Life in man and brute;
   Thou madest Death; and lo, thy foot
Is on the skull which thou hast made.

Thou wilt not leave us in the dust:
   Thou madest man, he knows not why,
   He thinks he was not made to die;
And thou hast made him: thou art just.

Thou seemest human and divine,
   The highest, holiest manhood, thou.
   Our wills are ours, we know not how;
Our wills are ours, to make them thine.

Our little systems have their day,
   They have their day and cease to be:
   They are but broken lights of thee,
And thou, O Lord, art more than they.

We have but faith: we cannot know;
   For knowledge is of things we see;
   And yet we trust it comes from thee,
A beam in darkness: let it grow.

Let knowledge grow from more to more,
   But more of reverence in us dwell;
   That mind and soul, according well,
May make one music as before,

But vaster. We are fools and slight;
   We mock thee when we do not fear:
   But help thy foolish ones to bear;
Help thy vain worlds to bear thy light.

Forgive what seem'd my sin in me;
   What seem'd my worth since I began;
   For merit lives from man to man,
And not from man, O Lord, to thee.

101

Forgive my grief for one removed,
   Thy creature, whom I found so fair.
   I trust he lives in thee, and there
I find him worthier to be loved.

40

Forgive these wild and wandering cries,
   Confusions of a wasted youth;
   Forgive them where they fail in truth,
And in thy wisdom make me wise.

I

I held it truth, with him who sings
   To one clear harp in divers tones,
   That men may rise on stepping stones
Of their dead selves to higher things.

But who shall so forecast the years
   And find in loss a gain to match?
   Or reach a hand thro' time to catch
The far-off interest of tears?

Let Love clasp Grief lest both be drown'd,
   Let darkness keep her raven gloss:
   Ah, sweeter to be drunk with loss,
To dance with death, to beat the ground,

10

Than that the victor Hours should scorn
   The long result of love, and boast,
   'Behold the man that loved and lost,
But all he was is overworn.'

II

Old yew, which graspest at the stones
   That name the under-lying dead,
   Thy fibres net the dreamless head,
Thy roots are wrapt about the bones.

The seasons bring the flower again,
   And bring the firstling to the flock;

And in the dusk of thee, the clock
Beats out the little lives of men.

O not for thee the glow, the bloom,
   Who changest not in any gale,
   Nor branding summer suns avail
To touch thy thousand years of gloom:

                                                    10

And gazing on thee, sullen tree,
   Sick for thy stubborn hardihood,
   I seem to fail from out my blood
And grow incorporate into thee.

VII

Dark, house, by which once more I stand
   Here in the long unlovely street,
   Doors, where my heart was used to beat
So quickly, waiting for a hand,

A hand that can be clasped no more –
   Behold me, for I cannot sleep,
   And like a guilty thing I creep
At earliest morning to the door.

He is not here; but far away
   The noise of life begins again,
   And ghastly through the drizzling rain
On the bald street breaks the blank day.

                                                    10

XLVIII

If these brief lays, of Sorrow born,
   Were taken to be such as closed
   Grave doubts and answers here proposed,
Then these were such as men might scorn:

Her care is not to part and prove;
   She takes, when harsher moods remit,
   What slender shade of doubt may flit,
And makes it vassal unto love:

103

And hence, indeed, she sports with words,
  But better serves a wholesome law,   10
  And holds it sin and shame to draw
The deepest measure from the chords:

Nor dare she trust a larger lay,
  But rather loosens from the lip
  Short swallow-flights of song, that dip
Their wings in tears, and skim away.

LIV

Oh yet we trust that somehow good
  Will be the final goal of ill,
  To pangs of nature, sins of will,
Defects of doubt, and taints of blood;

That nothing walks with aimless feet;
  That not one life shall be destroyed,
  Or cast as rubbish to the void,
When God hath made the pile complete;

That not a worm is cloven in vain;
  That not a moth with vain desire   10
  Is shrivelled in a fruitless fire,
Or but subserves another's gain.

Behold, we know not anything;
  I can but trust that good shall fall
  At last — far off — at last, to all,
And every winter change to spring.

So runs my dream: but what am I?
  An infant crying in the night:
  An infant crying for the light:
And with no language but a cry.

LV

The wish, that of the living whole
  No life may fail beyond the grave,

104

Derives it not from what we have
The likest God within the soul?

Are God and Nature then at strife,
    That Nature lends such evil dreams?
    So careful of the type she seems,
So careless of the single life;

That, I, considering everywhere
    Her secret meaning in her deeds,
    And finding that of fifty seeds
She often brings but one to bear,

10

I falter where I firmly trod,
    And falling with my weight of cares
    Upon the great world's altar-stairs
That slope through darkness up to God,

I stretch lame hands of faith, and grope,
    And gather dust and chaff, and call
    To what I feel is Lord of all,
And faintly trust the larger hope.

LVI

'So careful of the type?' but no.
    From scarpèd cliff and quarried stone
    She cries, 'A thousand types are gone:
I care for nothing, all shall go.

'Thou makest thine appeal to me:
    I bring to life, I bring to death:
    The spirit does but mean the breath:
I know no more.' And he, shall he,

Man, her last work, who seemed so fair,
    Such splendid purpose in his eyes,
    Who rolled the psalm to wintry skies,
Who built him fanes of fruitless prayer,

10

Who trusted God was love indeed
   And love Creation's final law –
   Though Nature, red in tooth and claw
With ravine, shriekced against his creed –

Who loved, who suffered countless ills,
   Who battled for the True, the Just,
   Be blown about the desert dust,
Or sealed within the iron hills?   20

No more? A monster then, a dream,
   A discord. Dragons of the prime,
   That tare each other in their slime,
Were mellow music matched with him.

O life as futile, then, as frail!
   O for thy voice to soothe and bless!
   What hope of answer, or redress?
Behind the veil, behind the veil.

XCV

By night we linger'd on the lawn,
   For underfoot the herb was dry;
   And genial warmth; and o'er the sky
The silvery haze of summer drawn;

And calm that let the tapers burn
   Unwavering: not a cricket chirr'd:
   The brook alone far-off was heard,
And on the board the fluttering urn.

And bats went round in fragrant skies,
   And wheel'd or lit the filmy shapes   10
   That haunt the dusk, with ermine capes
And woolly breasts and beaded eyes;

While now we sang old songs that peal'd
   From knoll to knoll, where, couch'd at ease,

The white kine glimmer'd, and the trees
Laid their dark arms about the field.

But when those others, one by one,
    Withdrew themselves from me and night,
    And in the house light after light
Went out, and I was all alone,   20

A hunger seized my heart; I read
    Of that glad year which once had been
    In those fall'n leaves which kept their green,
The noble letters of the dead:

And strangely on the silence broke
    The silent-speaking words, and strange
    Was love's dumb cry defying change
To test his worth; and strangely spoke

The faith, the vigour, bold to dwell
    On doubts that drive the coward back,   30
    And keen thro' wordy snares to track
Suggestion to her inmost cell.

So word by word, and line by line,
    The dead man touch'd me from the past,
    And all at once it seem'd at last
The living soul was flash'd on mine,

And mine in this was wound, and whirl'd
    About empyreal heights of thought,
    And came on that which is, and caught
The deep pulsations of the world,   40

Aeonian music measuring out
    The steps of Time – the shocks of Chance –
    The blows of Death. At length my trance
Was cancell'd, stricken thro' with doubt.

Vague words! but ah, how hard to frame
   In matter-moulded forms of speech,
   Or ev'n for intellect to reach
Thro' memory that which I became:

Till now the doubtful dusk reveal'd
   The knolls once more where, couch'd at ease,   50
   The white kine glimmer'd, and the trees
Laid their dark arms about the field:

And suck'd from out the distant gloom
   A breeze began to tremble o'er
   The large leaves of the sycamore,
And fluctuate all the still perfume,

And gathering freshlier overhead,
   Rock'd the full-foliaged elms, and swung
   The heavy-folded rose, and flung
The lilies to and fro, and said   60

'The dawn, the dawn,' and died away;
   And East and West, without a breath,
   Mixt their dim lights, like life and death,
To broaden into boundless day.

CIV

The time draws near the birth of Christ;
   The moon is hid, the night is still;
   A single church below the hill
Is pealing, folded in the mist.

A single peal of bells below,
   That wakens at this hour of rest
   A single murmur in the breast,
That these are not the bells I know.

Like strangers' voices here they sound,
   In lands where not a memory strays,   10
   Nor landmark breathes of other days,
But all is new unhallow'd ground.

CXXIII

There rolls the deep where grew the tree.
  O earth, what changes hast thou seen!
  There where the long street roars, hath been
The stillness of the central sea.

The hills are shadows, and they flow
  From form to form, and nothing stands:
  They melt like mist, the solid lands,
Like clouds they shape themselves and go.

But in my spirit will I dwell,
  And dream my dream, and hold it true;   10
  For tho' my lips may breathe adieu,
I cannot think the thing farewell.

CXXIX

Dear friend, far off, my lost desire,
  So far, so near in woe and weal;
  O loved the most, when most I feel
There is a lower and a higher;

Known and unknown; human, divine;
  Sweet human hand and lips and eye;
  Dear heavenly friend that canst not die,
Mine, mine, for ever, ever mine;

Strange friend, past, present, and to be;
  Loved deeplier, darklier understood;   10
  Behold, I dream a dream of good,
And mingle all the world with thee.

CXXXI

O living will that shalt endure
  When all that seems shall suffer shock,
  Rise in the spiritual rock,
Flow thro' our deeds and make them pure,

That we may lift from out of dust
  A voice as unto him that hears,

A cry above the conquer'd years
To one that with us works, and trust,

With faith that comes of self-control,
   The truths that never can be proved   10
   Until we close with all we loved,
And all we flow from, soul in soul.

ODE ON THE DEATH OF
THE DUKE OF WELLINGTON

I

Bury the Great Duke
   With an empire's lamentation,
Let us bury the Great Duke
   To the noise of the mourning of a mighty nation,
Mourning when their leaders fall,
Warriors carry the warrior's pall,
And sorrow darkens hamlet and hall.

II

Where shall we lay the man whom we deplore?
Here, in streaming London's central roar.
Let the sound of those he wrought for,   10
And the feet of those he fought for,
Echo round his bones for evermore.

III

Lead out the pageant: sad and slow,
As fits an universal woe,
Let the long long procession go,
And let the sorrowing crowd about it grow,
And let the mournful martial music blow;
The last great Englishman is low.

IV

Mourn, for to us he seems the last,
Remembering all his greatness in the Past.   20
No more in soldier fashion will he greet

With lifted hand the gazer in the street.
O friends, our chief state-oracle is mute:
Mourn for the man of long-enduring blood,
The statesman-warrior, moderate, resolute,
Whole in himself, a common good.
Mourn for the man of amplest influence,
Yet clearest of ambitious crime,
Our greatest yet with least pretence,
Great in council and great in war,   30
Foremost captain of his time,
Rich in saving common-sense,
And, as the greatest only are,
In his simplicity sublime.
O good gray head which all men knew,
O voice from which their omens all men drew,
O iron nerve to true occasion true,
O fall'n at length that tower of strength
Which stood four-square to all the winds that blew!
Such was he whom we deplore.   40
The long self-sacrifice of life is o'er.
The great World-victor's victor will be seen no more.

V

All is over and done:
Render thanks to the Giver,
England, for thy son.
Let the bell be toll'd.
Render thanks to the Giver,
And render him to the mould.
Under the cross of gold
That shines over city and river,   50
There he shall rest for ever
Among the wise and the bold.
Let the bell be toll'd:
And a reverent people behold
The towering car, the sable steeds:
Bright let it be with its blazon'd deeds,
Dark in its funeral fold.
Let the bell be toll'd:

And a deeper knell in the heart be knoll'd;
And the sound of the sorrowing anthem roll'd   60
Thro' the dome of the golden cross;
And the volleying cannon thunder his loss;
He knew their voices of old.
For many a time in many a clime
His captain's-ear has heard them boom
Bellowing victory, bellowing doom:
When he with those deep voices wrought,
Guarding realms and kings from shame;
With those deep voices our dead captain taught
The tyrant, and asserts his claim   70
In that dread sound to the great name,
Which he has worn so pure of blame,
In praise and in dispraise the same,
A man of well-attemper'd frame.
O civic muse, to such a name,
To such a name for ages long,
To such a name,
Preserve a broad approach of fame,
And ever-echoing avenues of song.

VI

Who is he that cometh, like an honour'd guest,   80
With banner and with music, with soldier and with priest,
With a nation weeping, and breaking on my rest?
Mighty Seaman, this is he
Was great by land as thou by sea.
Thine island loves thee well, thou famous man,
The greatest sailor since our world began.
Now, to the roll of muffled drums,
To thee the greatest soldier comes;
For this is he
Was great by land as thou by sea;   90
His foes were thine; he kept us free;
O give him welcome, this is he
Worthy of our gorgeous rites,
And worthy to be laid by thee;
For this is England's greatest son,

He that gain'd a hundred fights,
Nor ever lost an English gun;
This is he that far away
Against the myriads of Assaye
Clash'd with his fiery few and won;   100
And underneath another sun,
Warring on a later day,
Round affrighted Lisbon drew
The treble works, the vast designs
Of his labour'd rampart-lines,
Where he greatly stood at bay,
Whence he issued forth anew,
And ever great and greater grew,
Beating from the wasted vines
Back to France her banded swarms,   110
Back to France with countless blows,
Till o'er the hills her eagles flew
Beyond the Pyrenean pines,
Follow'd up in valley and glen
With blare of bugle, clamour of men,
Roll of cannon and clash of arms,
And England pouring on her foes.
Such a war had such a close.
Again their ravening eagle rose
In anger, wheel'd on Europe-shadowing wings,   120
And barking for the thrones of kings;
Till one that sought but Duty's iron crown
On that loud sabbath shook the spoiler down;
A day of onsets of despair!
Dash'd on every rocky square
Their surging charges foam'd themselves away;
Last, the Prussian trumpet blew;
Thro' the long-tormented air
Heaven flash'd a sudden jubilant ray,
And down we swept and charged and overthrew.   130
So great a soldier taught us there,
What long-enduring hearts could do
In that world-earthquake, Waterloo!
Mighty Seaman, tender and true,

And pure as he from taint of craven guile,
O saviour of the silver-coasted isle,
O shaker of the Baltic and the Nile,
If aught of things that here befall
Touch a spirit among things divine,
If love of country move thee there at all,
Be glad, because his bones are laid by thine!
And thro' the centuries let a people's voice
In full acclaim,
A people's voice,
The proof and echo of all human fame,
A people's voice, when they rejoice
At civic revel and pomp and game,
Attest their great commander's claim
With honour, honour, honour, honour to him,
Eternal honour to his name.   150

VII

A people's voice! we are a people yet.
Tho' all men else their nobler dreams forget,
Confused by brainless mobs and lawless Powers;
Thank Him who isled us here, and roughly set
His Briton in blown seas and storming showers,
We have a voice, with which to pay the debt,
Of boundless love and reverence and regret
To those great men who fought, and kept it ours.
And keep it ours, O God, from brute control;
O Statesmen, guard us, guard the eye, the soul   160
Of Europe, keep our noble England whole,
And save the one true seed of freedom sown
Betwixt a people and their ancient throne,
That sober freedom out of which there springs
Our loyal passion for our temperate kings;
For, saving that, ye help to save mankind
Till public wrong be crumbled into dust,
And drill the raw world for the march of mind,
Till crowds at length be sane and crowns be just.
But wink no more in slothful overtrust.   170
Remember him who led your hosts;

114

He bad you guard the sacred coasts.
Your cannons moulder on the seaward wall;
His voice is silent in your council-hall
For ever; and whatever tempests lour
For ever silent; even if they broke
In thunder, silent; yet remember all
He spoke among you, and the Man who spoke;
Who never sold the truth to serve the hour,
Nor palter'd with Eternal God for power;
Who let the turbid streams of rumour flow
Thro' either babbling world of high and low;
Whose life was work, whose language rife
With rugged maxims hewn from life;
Who never spoke against a foe;
Whose eighty winters freeze with one rebuke
All great self-seekers trampling on the right:
Truth-teller was our England's Alfred named;
Truth-lover was our English Duke;
Whatever record leap to light   190
He never shall be shamed.

VIII

Lo, the leader in these glorious wars
Now to glorious burial slowly borne,
Follow'd by the brave of other lands,
He, on whom from both her open hands
Lavish Honour shower'd all her stars,
And affluent Fortune emptied all her horn.
Yea, let all good things await
Him who cares not to be great,
But as he saves or serves the state.   200
Not once or twice in our rough island-story,
The path of duty was the way to glory:
He that walks it, only thirsting
For the right, and learns to deaden
Love of self, before his journey closes,
He shall find the stubborn thistle bursting
Into glossy purples, which outredden
All voluptuous garden-roses.

Not once or twice in our fair island-story,
The path of duty was the way to glory: 210
He, that ever following her commands,
On with toil of heart and knees and hands,
Thro' the long gorge to the far light has won
His path upward, and prevail'd,
Shall find the toppling crags of Duty scaled
Are close upon the shining table-lands
To which our God Himself is moon and sun.
Such was he: his work is done.
But while the races of mankind endure,
Let his great example stand   220
Colossal, seen of every land,
And keep the soldier firm, the statesman pure:
Till in all lands and thro' all human story
The path of duty be the way to glory:
And let the land whose hearths he saved from shame
For many and many an age proclaim
At civic revel and pomp and game,
And when the long-illumined cities flame,
Their ever-loyal iron leader's fame,
With honour, honour, honour, honour to him,   230
Eternal honour to his name.

IX

Peace, his triumph will be sung
By some yet unmoulded tongue
Far on in summers that we shall not see:
Peace, it is a day of pain
For one about whose patriarchal knee
Late the little children clung:
O peace, it is a day of pain
For one, upon whose hand and heart and brain
Once the weight and fate of Europe hung.   240
Ours the pain, be his the gain!
More than is of man's degree
Must be with us, watching here
At this, our great solemnity.
Whom we see not we revere;

We revere, and we refrain
From talk of battles loud and vain,
And brawling memories all too free
For such a wise humility
As befits a solemn fane: 250
We revere, and while we hear
The tides of Music's golden sea
Setting toward eternity,
Uplifted high in heart and hope are we,
Until we doubt not that for one so true
There must be other nobler work to do
Than when he fought at Waterloo,
And Victor he must ever be.
For tho' the Giant Ages heave the hill
And break the shore, and evermore   260
Make and break, and work their will;
Tho' world on world in myriad myriads roll
Round us, each with different powers,
And other forms of life than ours,
What know we greater than the soul?
On God and Godlike men we build our trust.
Hush, the Dead March wails in the people's ears:
The dark crowd moves, and there are sobs and tears:
The black earth yawns: the mortal disappears;
Ashes to ashes, dust to dust;   270
He is gone who seem'd so great –
Gone; but nothing can bereave him
Of the force he made his own
Being here, and we believe him
Something far advanced in State,
And that he wears a truer crown
Than any wreath that man can weave him.
Speak no more of his renown,
Lay your earthly fancies down,
And in the vast cathedral leave him.   280
God accept him, Christ receive him.

THE CHARGE OF THE LIGHT BRIGADE

I

Half a league, half a league,
  Half a league onward,
All in the valley of Death
  Rode the six hundred.
'Forward, the Light Brigade!
Charge for the guns!' he said:
Into the valley of Death
  Rode the six hundred.

II

'Forward, the Light Brigade!'
Was there a man dismay'd?   10
Not tho' the soldier knew
  Some one had blunder'd:
Their's not to make reply,
Their's not to reason why,
Their's but to do and die:
Into the valley of Death
  Rode the six hundred.

III

Cannon to right of them,
Cannon to left of them,
Cannon in front of them   20
  Volley'd and thunder'd;
Storm'd at with shot and shell,
Boldly they rode and well,
Into the jaws of Death,
Into the mouth of Hell
  Rode the six hundred.

IV

Flash'd all their sabres bare,
Flash'd as they turn'd in air
Sabring the gunners there,
Charging an army, while   30

All the world wonder'd:
Plunged in the battery-smoke
Right thro' the line they broke;
Cossack and Russian
Reel'd from the sabre-stroke
    Shatter'd and sunder'd.
Then they rode back, but not
    Not the six hundred.

V

Cannon to right of them,
Cannon to left of them,   40
Cannon behind them
    Volley'd and thunder'd;
Storm'd at with shot and shell,
While horse and hero fell,
They that had fought so well
Came thro' the jaws of Death,
Back from the mouth of Hell,
All that was left of them,
    Left of six hundred.

VI

When can their glory fade?   50
O the wild charge they made!
    All the world wonder'd.
Honour the charge they made!
Honour the Light Brigade,
    Noble six hundred!

From MAUD

A MONODRAMA

Part I

I

1

I hate the dreadful hollow behind the little wood,
Its lips in the field above are dabbled with blood-red heath,
The red-ribb'd ledges drip with a silent horror of blood,
And Echo there, whatever is ask'd her, answers 'Death.'

2

For there in the ghastly pit long since a body was found,
His who had given me life – O father! O God! was it well? –
Mangled, and flatten'd, and crush'd, and dinted into the
    ground:
There yet lies the rock that fell with him when he fell.

3

Did he fling himself down? who knows? for a vast speculation
    had fail'd,
And ever he mutter'd and madden'd, and ever wann'd with
    despair,   10
And out he walk'd when the wind like a broken worldling
    wail'd,
And the flying gold of the ruin'd woodlands drove thro' the air.

4

I remember the time, for the roots of my hair were stirr'd
By a shuffled step, by a dead weight trail'd, by a whisper'd fright,
And my pulses closed their gates with a shock on my heart as
    I heard
The shrill-edged shriek of a mother divide the shuddering night.

5

Villainy somewhere! whose? One says, we are villains all.
Not he: his honest fame should at least by me be maintain'd:

But that old man, now lord of the broad estate and the Hall,
Dropt off gorged from a scheme that had left us flaccid and
    drain'd.   20

6

Why do they prate of the blessings of Peace? we have made
    them a curse,
Pickpockets, each hand lusting for all that is not its own;
And lust of gain, in the spirit of Cain, is it better or worse
Than the heart of the citizen hissing in war on his own hearth-
    stone?

7

But these are the days of advance, the works of the men of mind,
When who but a fool would have faith in a tradesman's ware or
    his word?
Is it peace or war? Civil war, as I think, and that of a kind
The viler, as underhand, not openly bearing the sword.

8

Sooner or later I too may passively take the print
Of the golden age – why not? I have neither hope nor
    trust;   30
May make my heart as a millstone, set my face as a flint,
Cheat and be cheated, and die: who knows? we are ashes and
    dust.

9

Peace sitting under her olive, and slurring the days gone by,
When the poor are hovell'd and hustled together, each sex, like
    swine,
When only the ledger lives, and when only not all men lie;
Peace in her vineyard – yes! – but a company forges the wine.

10

And the vitriol madness flushes up in the ruffian's head,
Till the filthy by-lane rings to the yell of the trampled wife,
And chalk and alum and plaster are sold to the poor for bread,
And the spirit of murder works in the very means of life.   40

11

And Sleep must lie down arm'd, for the villainous centre-bits
Grind on the wakeful ear in the hush of the moonless nights,
While another is cheating the sick of a few last gasps, as he sits
To pestle a poison'd poison behind his crimson lights.

12

When a Mammonite mother kills her babe for a burial fee,
And Timour-Mammon grins on a pile of children's bones,
Is it peace or war? better, war! loud war by land and by sea,
War with a thousand battles, and shaking a hundred thrones.

13

For I trust if an enemy's fleet came yonder round by the hill,
And the rushing battle-bolt sang from the three-decker out
    of the foam,   50
That the smoothfaced snubnosed rogue would leap from his
    counter and till,
And strike, if he could, were it but with his cheating yardwand,
    home.

14

What! am I raging alone as my father raged in his mood?
Must *I* too creep to the hollow and dash myself down and die
Rather than hold by the law that I made, nevermore to brood
On a horror of shatter'd limbs and a wretched swindler's lie?

15

Would there be sorrow for *me*? there was *love* in the passionate
    shriek,
Love for the silent thing that had made false haste to the grave –
Wrapt in a cloak, as I saw him, and thought he would rise and
    speak
And rave at the lie and the liar, ah God, as he used to rave.   60

16

I am sick of the Hall and the hill, I am sick of the moor and the
    main.
Why should I stay? can a sweeter chance ever come to me here?

O, having the nerves of motion as well as the nerves of pain,
Were it not wise if I fled from the place and the pit and the fear?

17

Workmen up at the Hall! – they are coming back from abroad;
The dark old place will be gilt by the touch of a millionaire:
I have heard, I know not whence, of the singular beauty of
    Maud;
I play'd with the girl when a child; she promised then to be
    fair.

18

Maud with her venturous climbings and tumbles and childish
    escapes,
Maud the delight of the village, the ringing joy of the Hall,   70
Maud with her sweet purse-mouth when my father dangled the
    grapes,
Maud the beloved of my mother, the moon-faced darling of all, –

19

What is she now? My dreams are bad. She may bring me a curse,
No, there is fatter game on the moor; she will let me alone.
Thanks, for the fiend best knows whether woman or man be
    the worse.
I will bury myself in myself, and the Devil may pipe to his
    own.

IV

5

We are puppets, Man in his pride, and Beauty fair in her
    flower;
Do we move ourselves, or are moved by an unseen hand at a
    game
That pushes us off from the board, and others ever succeed?
Ah yet, we cannot be kind to each other here for an hour;
We whisper, and hint, and chuckle, and grin at a brother's
    shame;
However we brave it out, we men are a little breed.

6

A monstrous eft was of old the Lord and Master of Earth,
For him did his high sun flame, and his river billowing ran,
And he felt himself in his force to be Nature's crowning race.
As nine months go to the shaping an infant ripe for his birth,   10
So many a million of ages have gone to the making of man:
He now is first, but is he the last? is he not too base?

XX

1

Strange, that I felt so gay,
Strange, that I tried to-day
To beguile her melancholy;
The Sultan, as we name him, –
She did not wish to blame him –
But he vext her and perplext her
With his wordly talk and folly:
Was it gentle to reprove her
For stealing out of view
From a little lazy lover
Who but claims her as his due?   10
Or for chilling his caresses
By the coldness of her manners,
Nay, the plainness of her dresses?
Now I know her but in two,
Nor can pronounce upon it
If one should ask me whether
The habit, hat, and feather,
Or the frock and gipsy bonnet
Be the neater and completer;   20
For nothing can be sweeter
Than maiden Maud in either.

2

But to morrow, if we live,
Our ponderous squire will give
A grand political dinner
To half the squirelings near;

And Maud will wear her jewels,
And the bird of prey will hover,
And the titmouse hope to win her
With his chirrup at her ear.   30

                    3

A grand political dinner
To the men of many acres,
A gathering of the Tory,
A dinner and then a dance
For the maids and marriage-makers,
And every eye but mine will glance
At Maud in all her glory.

                    4

For I am not invited,
But, with the Sultan's pardon,
I am all as well delighted,   40
For I know her own rose-garden,
And mean to linger in it
Till the dancing will be over;
And then, oh then, come out to me
For a minute, but for a minute,
Come out to your own true lover,
That your true lover may see
Your glory also, and render
All homage to his own darling,
Queen Maud in all her splendour.   50

                    XXI

Rivulet crossing my ground,
And bringing me down from the Hall
This garden-rose that I found,
Forgetful of Maud and me,
And lost in trouble and moving round
Here at the head of a tinkling fall,
And trying to pass to the sea;
O Rivulet, born at the Hall,
My Maud has sent it by thee

125

(If I read her sweet will right)   10
On a blushing mission to me,
Saying in odour and colour, 'Ah, be
Among the roses to-night.'

XXII

1

Come into the garden, Maud,
  For the black bat, night, has flown,
Come into the garden, Maud,
  I am here at the gate alone;
And the woodbine spices are wafted abroad,
  And the musk of the rose is blown.

2

For a breeze of morning moves,
  And the planet of Love is on high,
Beginning to faint in the light that she loves
  On a bed of daffodil sky,   10
To faint in the light of the sun she loves,
  To faint in his light, and to die.

3

All night have the roses heard
  The flute, violin, bassoon;
All night has the casement jessamine stirr'd
  To the dancers dancing in tune;
Till a silence fell with the waking bird,
  And a hush with the setting moon.

4

I said to the lily, 'There is but one
  With whom she has heart to be gay.
When will the dancers leave her alone?   20
  She is weary of dance and play.'
Now half to the setting moon are gone,
  And half to the rising day;
Low on the sand and loud on the stone
  The last wheel echoes away.

5

I said to the rose, 'The brief night goes
    In babble and revel and wine.
O young lord-lover, what sighs are those,
    For one that will never be thine?   30
But mine, but mine,' so I sware to the rose,
    'For ever and ever, mine.'

6

And the soul of the rose went into my blood,
    As the music clash'd in the hall;
And long by the garden lake I stood,
    For I heard your rivulet fall
From the lake to the meadow and on to the wood,
    Our wood, that is dearer than all;

7

From the meadow your walks have left so sweet
    That whenever a March-wind sighs   40
He sets the jewel-print of your feet
    In violets blue as your eyes,
To the woody hollows in which we meet
    And the valleys of Paradise.

8

The slender acacia would not shake
    One long milk-bloom on the tree;
The white lake-blossom fell into the lake,
    As the pimpernel dozed on the lea;
But the rose was awake all night for your sake,
    Knowing your promise to me;   50
The lilies and roses were all awake,
    They sigh'd for the dawn and thee.

9

Queen rose of the rosebud garden of girls,
    Come hither, the dances are done,
In gloss of satin and glimmer of pearls,
    Queen lily and rose in one;

Shine out, little head, sunning over with curls,
   To the flowers, and be their sun.

10

There has fallen a splendid tear
   From the passion-flower at the gate.
She is coming, my dove, my dear;
   She is coming, my life, my fate;
The red rose cries, 'She is near, she is near;'
   And the white rose weeps, 'She is late;'
The larkspur listens, 'I hear, I hear;'
   And the lily whispers, 'I wait.'   60

11

She is coming, my own, my sweet;
   Were it ever so airy a tread,
My heart would hear her and beat,
   Were it earth in an earthy bed;
My dust would hear her and beat,
   Had I lain for a century dead;
Would start and tremble under her feet,
   And blossom in purple and red.   70

Part II

I

1

'The fault was mine, the fault was mine' –
Why am I sitting here so stunn'd and still,
Plucking the harmless wild-flower on the hill? –
It is this guilty hand! –
And there rises ever a passionate cry
From underneath in the darkening land –
What is it, that has been done?
O dawn of Eden bright over earth and sky,
The fires of Hell brake out of thy rising sun,
The fires of Hell and of Hate;   10
For she, sweet soul, had hardly spoken a word,

128

When her brother ran in his rage to the gate,
He came with the babe-faced lord;
Heap'd on her terms of disgrace,
And while she wept, and I strove to be cool,
He fiercely gave me the lie,
Till I with as fierce an anger spoke,
And he struck me, madman, over the face,
Struck me before the languid fool,
Who was gaping and grinning by: 20
Struck for himself an evil stroke;
Wrought for his house an irredeemable woe;
For front to front in an hour we stood,
And a million horrible bellowing echoes broke
From the red-ribb'd hollow behind the wood,
And thunder'd up into Heaven the Christless code,
That must have life for a blow.
Ever and ever afresh they seem'd to grow.
Was it he lay there with a fading eye?
'The fault was mine,' he whisper'd, 'fly!'   30
Then glided out of the joyous wood
The ghastly Wraith of one that I know;
And there rang on a sudden a passionate cry,
A cry for a brother's blood:
It will ring in my heart and my ears, till I die, till I die.

2

Is it gone? my pulses beat –
What was it? a lying trick of the brain?
Yet I thought I saw her stand,
A shadow there at my feet,
High over the shadowy land.   40
It is gone; and the heavens fall in a gentle rain,
When they should burst and drown with deluging storms
The feeble vassals of wine and anger and lust,
The little hearts that know not how to forgive:
Arise, my God, and strike, for we hold Thee just,
Strike dead the whole weak race of venomous worms,
That sting each other here in the dust;
We are not worthy to live.

II

1

See what a lovely shell,
Small and pure as a pearl,
Lying close to my foot,
Frail, but a work divine,
Made so fairily well
With delicate spire and whorl,
How exquisitely minute,
A miracle of design!

2

What is it? a learned man
Could give it a clumsy name.   10
Let him name it who can,
The beauty would be the same.

3

The tiny cell is forlorn,
Void of the little living will
That made it stir on the shore.
Did he stand at the diamond door
Of his house in a rainbow frill?
Did he push, when he was uncurl'd,
A golden foot or a fairy horn
Thro' his dim water-world?   20

4

Slight, to be crush'd with a tap
Of my finger-nail on the sand,
Small, but a work divine,
Frail, but of force to withstand,
Year upon year, the shock
Of cataract seas that snap
The three-decker's oaken spine
Athwart the ledges of rock,
Here on the Breton strand!

5

Breton, not Briton; here 30
Like a shipwreck'd man on a coast
Of ancient fable and fear –
Plagued with a flitting to and fro,
A disease; a hard mechanic ghost
That never came from on high
Nor ever arose from below,
But only moves with the moving eye,
Flying along the land and the main –
Why should it look like Maud? 40
Am I to be overawed
By what I cannot but know
Is a juggle born of the brain?

6

Back from the Breton coast,
Sick of a nameless fear,
Back to the dark sea-line
Looking, thinking of all I have lost;
An old song vexes my ear;
But that of Lamech is mine.

7

For years, a measureless ill, 50
For years, for ever, to part –
But she, she would love me still;
And as long, O God, as she
Have a grain of love for me,
So long, no doubt, no doubt,
Shall I nurse in my dark heart,
However weary, a spark of will
Not to be trampled out.

8

Strange, that the mind, when fraught
With a passion so intense
One would think that it well 60
Might drown all life in the eye, –

131

That it should, by being so overwrought,
Suddenly strike on a sharper sense
For a shell, or a flower, little things
Which else would have been past by!
And now I remember, I,
When he lay dying there,
I noticed one of his many rings
(For he had many, poor worm) and thought
It is his mother's hair.   70

9

Who knows if he be dead?
Whether I need have fled?
Am I guilty of blood?
However this may be,
Comfort her, comfort her, all things good,
While I am over the sea!
Let me and my passionate love go by,
But speak to her all things holy and high,
Whatever happen to me!
Me and my harmful love go by;   80
But come to her waking, find her asleep,
Powers of the height, Powers of the deep,
And comfort her tho' I die.

IV

1

O that 'twere possible
After long grief and pain
To find the arms of my true love
Round me once again!

2

When I was wont to meet her
In the silent woody places
By the home that gave me birth,
We stood tranced in long embraces
Mixt with kisses sweeter sweeter
Than any thing on earth.   10

3

A shadow flits before me,
Not thou, but like to thee;
Ah Christ, that it were possible
For one short hour to see
The souls we loved, that they might tell us
What and where they be.

4

It leads me forth at evening,
It lightly winds and steals
In a cold white robe before me,
When all my spirit reels   20
At the shouts, the leagues of lights,
And the roaring of the wheels.

5

Half the night I waste in sighs,
Half in dreams I sorrow after
The delight of early skies;
In a wakeful doze I sorrow
For the hand, the lips, the eyes,
For the meeting of the morrow,
The delight of happy laughter,
The delight of low replies.   30

6

'Tis a morning pure and sweet,
And a dewy splendour falls
On the little flower that clings
To the turrets and the walls;
'Tis a morning pure and sweet,
And the light and shadow fleet;
She is walking in the meadow,
And the woodland echo rings;
In a moment we shall meet;
She is singing in the meadow,   40
And the rivulet at her feet
Ripples on in light and shadow
To the ballad that she sings.

7

Do I hear her sing as of old,
My bird with the shining head,
My own dove with the tender eye?
But there rings on a sudden a passionate cry
There is some one dying or dead,
And a sullen thunder is roll'd;
For a tumult shakes the city,   50
And I wake, my dream is fled;
In the shuddering dawn, behold,
Without knowledge, without pity,
By the curtains of my bed
That abiding phantom cold.

8

Get thee hence, nor come again,
Mix not memory with doubt,
Pass, thou deathlike type of pain,
Pass and cease to move about,
'Tis the blot upon the brain   60
That *will* show itself without.

9

Then I rise, the eavedrops fall,
And the yellow vapours choke
The great city sounding wide;
The day comes, a dull red ball
Wrapt in drifts of lurid smoke
On the misty river-tide.

10

Thro' the hubbub of the market
I steal, a wasted frame,
It crosses here, it crosses there,   70
Thro' all that crowd confused and loud,
The shadow still the same;
And on my heavy eyelids
My anguish hangs like shame.

134

11

Alas for her that met me,
That heard me softly call,
Came glimmering thro' the laurels
At the quiet evenfall,
In the garden by the turrets
Of the old manorial hall.

80

12

Would the happy spirit descend,
From the realms of light and song,
In the chamber or the street,
As she looks among the blest,
Should I fear to greet my friend
Or to say 'forgive the wrong,'
Or to ask her, 'take me, sweet,
To the regions of thy rest?'

13

But the broad light glares and beats,
And the shadow flits and fleets

90

And will not let me be;
And I loathe the squares and streets,
And the faces that one meets,
Hearts with no love for me:
Always I long to creep
Into some still cavern deep,
There to weep, and weep, and weep
My whole soul out to thee.

Part III

VI

1

My life has crept so long on a broken wing
Thro' cells of madness, haunts of horror and fear,
That I come to be grateful at last for a little thing:
My mood is changed, for it fell at a time of year

When the face of night is fair on the dewy downs,
And the shining daffodil dies, and the Charioteer
And starry Gemini hang like glorious crowns
Over Orion's grave low down in the west,
That like a silent lightning under the stars
She seem'd to divide in a dream from a band of the blest,   10
And spoke of a hope for the world in the coming wars –
'And in that hope, dear soul, let trouble have rest,
Knowing I tarry for thee,' and pointed to Mars
As he glow'd like a ruddy shield on the Lion's breast.

2

And it was but a dream, yet it yielded a dear delight
To have look'd, tho' but in a dream, upon eyes so fair,
That had been in a weary world my one thing bright;
And it was but a dream, yet it lighten'd my despair
When I thought that a war would arise in defence of the right,
That an iron tyranny now should bend or cease,   20
The glory of manhood stand on his ancient height,
Nor Britain's one sole God be the millionaire:
No more shall commerce be all in all, and Peace
Pipe on her pastoral hillock a languid note,
And watch her harvest ripen, her herd increase,
Nor the cannon-bullet rust on a slothful shore,
And the cobweb woven across the cannon's throat
Shall shake its threaded tears in the wind no more.

3

And as months ran on and rumour of battle grew,
'It is time, it is time, O passionate heart,' said I   30
(For I cleaved to a cause that I felt to be pure and true),
'It is time, O passionate heart and morbid eye,
That old hysterical mock-disease should die.'
And I stood on a giant deck and mix'd my breath
With a loyal people shouting a battle cry,
Till I saw the dreary phantom arise and fly
Far into the North, and battle, and seas of death.

4

Let it go or stay, so I wake to the higher aims
Of a land that has lost for a little her lust of gold,
And love of a peace that was full of wrongs and shames,   40
Horrible, hateful, monstrous, not to be told;
And hail once more to the banner of battle unroll'd!
Tho' many a light shall darken, and many shall weep
For those that are crush'd in the clash of jarring claims,
Yet God's just wrath shall be wreak'd on a giant liar;
And many a darkness into the light shall leap,
And shine in the sudden making of splendid names,
And noble thought be freer under the sun,
And the heart of a people beat with one desire;
For the peace, that I deemed no peace, is over and done,   50
And now by the side of the Black and the Baltic deep,
And deathful-grinning mouths of the fortress, flames
The blood-red blossom of war with a heart of fire.

5

Let it flame or fade, and the war roll down like a wind,
We have proved we have hearts in a cause, we are noble still,
And myself have awaked, as it seems, to the better mind;
It is better to fight for the good than to rail at the ill;
I have felt with my native land, I am one with my kind,
I embrace the purpose of God, and the doom assigned.

TITHONUS

The woods decay, the woods decay and fall,
The vapours weep their burthen to the ground,
Man comes and tills the field and lies beneath,
And after many a summer dies the swan.
Me only cruel immortality
Consumes: I wither slowly in thine arms,
Here at the quiet limit of the world,
A white-hair'd shadow roaming like a dream
The ever-silent spaces of the East,
Far-folded mists, and gleaming halls of morn.   10

Alas! for this gray shadow, once a man –
So glorious in his beauty and thy choice,
Who madest him thy chosen, that he seem'd
To his great heart none other than a God!
I ask'd thee, 'Give me immortality.'
Then didst thou grant mine asking with a smile,
Like wealthy men who care not how they give.
But thy strong Hours indignant work'd their wills,
And beat me down and marr'd and wasted me,
And tho' they could not end me, left me maim'd   20
To dwell in presence of immortal youth,
Immortal age beside immortal youth,
And all I was, in ashes. Can thy love,
Thy beauty, make amends, tho' even now,
Close over us, the silver star, thy guide,
Shines in those tremulous eyes that fill with tears
To hear me? Let me go: take back thy gift:
Why should a man desire in any way
To vary from the kindly race of men,
Or pass beyond the goal of ordinance   30
Where all should pause, as is most meet for all?

A soft air fans the cloud apart; there comes
A glimpse of that dark world where I was born.
Once more the old mysterious glimmer steals
From thy pure brows, and from thy shoulders pure,
And bosom beating with a heart renew'd.
Thy cheek begins to redden thro' the gloom,
Thy sweet eyes brighten slowly close to mine,
Ere yet they blind the stars, and the wild team
Which love thee, yearning for thy yoke, arise,   40
And shake the darkness from their loosen'd manes,
And beat the twilight into flakes of fire.

Lo! ever thus thou growest beautiful
In silence, then before thine answer given
Departest, and thy tears are on my cheek.

138

Why wilt thou ever scare me with thy tears,
And make me tremble lest a saying learnt,
In days far-off, on that dark earth, be true?
'The Gods themselves cannot recall their gifts.'

Ay me! ay me! with what another heart   50
In days far-off, and with what other eyes
I used to watch – if I be he that watch'd –
The lucid outline forming round thee; saw
The dim curls kindle into sunny rings;
Changed with thy mystic change, and felt my blood
Glow with the glow that slowly crimson'd all
Thy presence and thy portals, while I lay,
Mouth, forehead, eyelids, growing dewy-warm
With kisses balmier than half-opening buds
Of April, and could hear the lips that kiss'd   60
Whispering I knew not what of wild and sweet,
Like that strange song I heard Apollo sing,
While Ilion like a mist rose into towers.
Yet hold me not for ever in thine East:
How can my nature longer mix with thine?
Coldly thy rosy shadows bathe me, cold
Are all thy lights, and cold my wrinkled feet
Upon thy glimmering thresholds, when the steam
Floats up from those dim fields about the homes
Of happy men that have the power to die,   70
And grassy barrows of the happier dead.
Release me, and restore me to the ground;
Thou seëst all things, thou wilt see my grave:
Thou wilt renew thy beauty morn by morn;
I earth in earth forget these empty courts,
And thee returning on thy silver wheels.

139

IN THE VALLEY OF CAUTERETZ

All along the valley, stream that flashest white,
Deepening thy voice with the deepening of the night,
All along the valley, where thy waters flow,
I walk'd with one I loved two and thirty years ago.
All along the valley, while I walk'd to-day,
The two and thirty years were a mist that rolls away;
For all along the valley, down thy rocky bed,
Thy living voice to me was as the voice of the dead,
And all along the valley, by rock and cave and tree,
The voice of the dead was a living voice to me.

ENOCH ARDEN

Long lines of cliff breaking have left a chasm;
And in the chasm are foam and yellow sands;
Beyond, red roofs about a narrow wharf
In cluster; then a moulder'd church; and higher
A long street climbs to one tall-tower'd mill;
And high in heaven behind it a gray down
With Danish barrows; and a hazelwood,
By autumn nutters haunted, flourishes
Green in a cuplike hollow of the down.

Here on this beach a hundred years ago,   10
Three children of three houses, Annie Lee,
The prettiest little damsel in the port,
And Philip Ray the miller's only son,
And Enoch Arden, a rough sailor's lad
Made orphan by a winter shipwreck, play'd
Among the waste and lumber of the shore,
Hard coils of cordage, swarthy fishing-nets,
Anchors of rusty fluke, and boats updrawn;
And built their castles of dissolving sand
To watch them overflow'd, or following up   20
And flying the white breaker, daily left
The little footprint daily wash'd away.

140

A narrow cave ran in beneath the cliff:
In this the children play'd at keeping house.
Enoch was host one day, Philip the next,
While Annie still was mistress; but at times
Enoch would hold possession for a week:
'This is my house and this my little wife.'
'Mine too' said Philip 'turn and turn about:'
When, if they quarrell'd, Enoch stronger-made   30
Was master: then would Philip, his blue eyes
All flooded with the helpless wrath of tears,
Shriek out 'I hate you, Enoch,' and at this
The little wife would weep for company,
And pray them not to quarrel for her sake,
And say she would be little wife to both.

But when the dawn of rosy childhood past,
And the new warmth of life's ascending sun
Was felt by either, either fixt his heart
On that one girl; and Enoch spoke his love,   40
But Philip loved in silence; and the girl
Seem'd kinder unto Philip than to him;
But she loved Enoch; tho' she knew it not,
And would if ask'd deny it. Enoch set
A purpose evermore before his eyes,
To hoard all savings to the uttermost,
To purchase his own boat, and make a home
For Annie: and so prosper'd that at last
A luckier or a bolder fisherman,
A carefuller in peril, did not breathe   50
For leagues along that breaker-beaten coast
Than Enoch. Likewise had he served a year
On board a merchantman, and made himself
Full sailor; and he thrice had pluck'd a life
From the dread sweep of the down-streaming seas:
And all men look'd upon him favourably:
And ere he touch'd his one-and-twentieth May
He purchased his own boat, and made a home
For Annie, neat and nestlike, halfway up
The narrow street that clamber'd toward the mill.   60

141

Then, on a golden autumn eventide,
The younger people making holiday,
With bag and sack and basket, great and small,
Went nutting to the hazels. Philip stay'd
(His father lying sick and needing him)
An hour behind; but as he climb'd the hill,
Just where the prone edge of the wood began
To feather toward the hollow, saw the pair,
Enoch and Annie, sitting hand-in-hand,
His large gray eyes and weather-beaten face   70
All-kindled by a still and sacred fire,
That burn'd as on an altar. Philip look'd,
And in their eyes and faces read his doom;
Then, as their faces drew together, groan'd,
And slipt aside, and like a wounded life
Crept down into the hollows of the wood;
There, while the rest were loud in merrymaking,
Had his dark hour unseen, and rose and past
Bearing a lifelong hunger in his heart.

So these were wed, and merrily rang the bells,   80
And merrily ran the years, seven happy years,
Seven happy years of health and competence,
And mutual love and honourable toil;
With children; first a daughter. In him woke,
With his first babe's first cry, the noble wish
To save all earnings to the uttermost,
And give his child a better bringing-up
Than his had been, or hers; a wish renew'd,
When two years after came a boy to be
The rosy idol of her solitudes,   90
While Enoch was abroad on wrathful seas,
Or often journeying landward; for in truth
Enoch's white horse, and Enoch's ocean-spoil
In ocean-smelling osier, and his face,
Rough-redden'd with a thousand winter gales,
Not only to the market-cross were known,
But in the leafy lanes behind the down,
Far as the portal-warding lion-whelp,

And peacock-yewtree of the lonely Hall,
Whose Friday fare was Enoch's ministering.   100

Then came a change, as all things human change.
Ten miles to northward of the narrow port
Open'd a larger haven: thither used
Enoch at times to go by land or sea;
And once when there, and clambering on a mast
In harbour, by mischance he slipt and fell:
A limb was broken when they lifted him;
And while he lay recovering there, his wife
Bore him another son, a sickly one:
Another hand crept too across his trade   110
Taking her bread and theirs: and on him fell,
Altho' a grave and staid God-fearing man,
Yet lying thus inactive, doubt and gloom.
He seem'd, as in a nightmare of the night,
To see his children leading evermore
Low miserable lives of hand-to-mouth,
And her, he loved, a beggar: then he pray'd
'Save them from this, whatever comes to me.'
And while he pray'd, the master of that ship
Enoch had served in, hearing his mischance,   120
Came, for he knew the man and valued him,
Reporting of his vessel China-bound,
And wanting yet a boatswain. Would he go?
There yet were many weeks before she sail'd,
Sail'd from this port. Would Enoch have the place?
And Enoch all at once assented to it,
Rejoicing at that answer to his prayer.

So now that shadow of mischance appear'd
No graver than as when some little cloud
Cuts off the fiery highway of the sun,   130
And isles a light in the offing: yet the wife –
When he was gone – the children – what to do?
Then Enoch lay long-pondering on his plans;
To sell the boat – and yet he loved her well –
How many a rough sea had he weather'd in her!

143

He knew her, as a horseman knows his horse —
And yet to sell her — then with what she brought
Buy goods and stores — set Annie forth in trade.
With all that seamen needed or their wives —
So might she keep the house while he was gone.   140
Should he not trade himself out yonder? go
This voyage more than once? yea twice or thrice —
As oft as needed — last, returning rich,
Become the master of a larger craft,
With fuller profits lead an easier life,
Have all his pretty young ones educated,
And pass his days in peace among his own.

Thus Enoch in his heart determined all:
Then moving homeward came on Annie pale,
Nursing the sickly babe, her latest-born.   150
Forward she started with a happy cry,
And laid the feeble infant in his arms;
Whom Enoch took, and handled all his limbs,
Appraised his weight and fondled fatherlike,
But had no heart to break his purposes
To Annie, till the morrow, when he spoke.

Then first since Enoch's golden ring had girt
Her finger, Annie fought against his will:
Yet not with brawling opposition she,
But manifold entreaties, many a tear,   160
Many a sad kiss by day by night renew'd
(Sure that all evil would come out of it)
Besought him, supplicating, if he cared
For her or his dear children, not to go.
He not for his own self caring but her,
Her and her children, let her plead in vain;
So grieving held his will, and bore it thro'.

For Enoch parted with his old sea-friend,
Bought Annie goods and stores, and set his hand
To fit their little streetward sitting-room   170
With shelf and corner for the goods and stores.

So all day long till Enoch's last at home,
Shaking their pretty cabin, hammer and axe,
Auger and saw, while Annie seem'd to hear
Her own death-scaffold raising, shrill'd and rang,
Till this was ended, and his careful hand, –
The space was narrow, – having order'd all
Almost as neat and close as Nature packs
Her blossom or her seedling, paused; and he,
Who needs would work for Annie to the last,   180
Ascending tired, heavily slept till morn.

And Enoch faced this morning of farewell
Brightly and boldly. All his Annie's fears,
Save, as his Annie's, were a laughter to him.
Yet Enoch as a brave God-fearing man
Bow'd himself down, and in that mystery
Where God-in-man is one with man-in-God,
Pray'd for a blessing on his wife and babes
Whatever came to him: and then he said
'Annie, this voyage by the grace of God   190
Will bring fair weather yet to all of us.
Keep a clean hearth and a clear fire for me,
For I'll be back, my girl, before you know it.'
Then lightly rocking baby's cradle 'and he,
This pretty, puny, weakly little one, –
Nay – for I love him all the better for it –
God bless him, he shall sit upon my knees
And I will tell him tales of foreign parts,
And make him merry, when I come home again.
Come Annie, come, cheer up before I go.'   200

Him running on thus hopefully she heard,
And almost hoped herself; but when he turn'd
The current of his talk to graver things
In sailor fashion roughly sermonizing
On providence and trust in Heaven, she heard,
Heard and not heard him; as the village girl,
Who sets her pitcher underneath the spring,
Musing on him that used to fill it for her,
Hears and not hears, and lets it overflow.

At length she spoke 'O Enoch, you are wise;   210
And yet for all your wisdom well know I
That I shall look upon your face no more.'

'Well then,' said Enoch, 'I shall look on yours.
Annie, the ship I sail in passes here
(He named the day) get you a seaman's glass,
Spy out my face, and laugh at all your fears.'

But when the last of those last moments came,
'Annie, my girl, cheer up, be comforted,
Look to the babes, and till I come again,
Keep everything shipshape, for I must go.   220
And fear no more for me; or if you fear
Cast all your cares on God; that anchor holds.
Is He not yonder in those uttermost
Parts of the morning? if I flee to these
Can I go from Him? and the sea is His,
The sea is His: He made it.'
                              Enoch rose,
Cast his strong arms about his drooping wife,
And kiss'd his wonder-stricken little ones;
But for the third, the sickly one, who slept
After a night of feverous wakefulness,   230
When Annie would have raised him Enoch said
'Wake him not; let him sleep; how should the child
Remember this?' and kiss'd him in his cot.
But Annie from her baby's forehead clipt
A tiny curl, and gave it: this he kept
Thro' all his future; but now hastily caught
His bundle, waved his hand, and went his way.

She when the day, that Enoch mention'd, came,
Borrow'd a glass, but all in vain: perhaps
She could not fix the glass to suit her eye;   240
Perhaps her eye was dim, hand tremulous;
She saw him not: and while he stood on deck
Waving, the moment and the vessel past.

146

Ev'n to the last dip of the vanishing sail
She watch'd it, and departed weeping for him;
Then, tho' she mourn'd his absence as his grave,
Set her sad will no less to chime with his,
But throve not in her trade, not being bred
To barter, nor compensating the want
By shrewdness, neither capable of lies,   250
Nor asking overmuch and taking less,
And still foreboding 'what would Enoch say?'
For more than once, in days of difficulty
And pressure, had she sold her wares for less
Than what she gave in buying what she sold:
She fail'd and sadden'd knowing it; and thus,
Expectant of that news which never came,
Gain'd for her own a scanty sustenance,
And lived a life of silent melancholy.

Now the third child was sickly-born and grew   260
Yet sicklier, tho' the mother cared for it
With all a mother's care: nevertheless,
Whether her business often call'd her from it,
Or thro' the want of what it needed most,
Or means to pay the voice who best could tell
What most it needed – howsoe'er it was,
After a lingering, – ere she was aware, –
Like the caged bird escaping suddenly,
The little innocent soul flitted away.

In that same week when Annie buried it,   270
Philip's true heart, which hunger'd for her peace
(Since Enoch left he had not look'd upon her),
Smote him, as having kept aloof so long.
'Surely' said Philip 'I may see her now,
May be some little comfort;' therefore went,
Past thro' the solitary room in front,
Paused for a moment at an inner door,
Then struck it thrice, and, no one opening,
Enter'd; but Annie, seated with her grief,
Fresh from the burial of her little one,   280
Cared not to look on any human face,

But turn'd her own toward the wall and wept.
Then Philip standing up said falteringly
'Annie, I came to ask a favour of you.'

He spoke; the passion in her moan'd reply
'Favour from one so sad and so forlorn
As I am!' half abash'd him; yet unask'd,
His bashfulness and tenderness at war,
He set himself beside her, saying to her:

'I came to speak to you of what he wish'd,   290
Enoch, your husband: I have ever said
You chose the best among us — a strong man:
For where he fixt his heart he set his hand
To do the thing he will'd, and bore it thro'.
And wherefore did he go this weary way,
And leave you lonely? not to see the world —
For pleasure? — nay, but for the wherewithal
To give his babes a better bringing-up
Than his had been, or yours: that was his wish.
And if he come again, vext will he be   300
To find the precious morning hours were lost.
And it would vex him even in his grave,
If he could know his babes were running wild
Like colts about the waste. So, Annie, now —
Have we not known each other all our lives?
I do beseech you by the love you bear
Him and his children not to say me nay —
For, if you will, when Enoch comes again
Why then he shall repay me — if you will,
Annie — for I am rich and well-to-do.   310
Now let me put the boy and girl to school:
This is the favour that I came to ask.

Then Annie with her brows against the wall
Answer'd 'I cannot look you in the face;
I seem so foolish and so broken down.
When you came in my sorrow broke me down;
And now I think your kindness breaks me down;

148

But Enoch lives; that is borne in on me:
He will repay you: money can be repaid;
Not kindness such as yours.'

                And Philip ask'd   320
'Then you will let me, Annie?'

                    There she turn'd,
She rose, and fixt her swimming eyes upon him,
And dwelt a moment on his kindly face,
Then calling down a blessing on his head
Caught at his hand, and wrung it passionately,
And past into the little garth beyond.
So lifted up in spirit he moved away.

   Then Philip put the boy and girl to school,
And bought them needful books, and everyway,
Like one who does his duty by his own,   330
Made himself theirs; and tho' for Annie's sake,
Fearing the lazy gossip of the port,
He oft denied his heart his dearest wish,
And seldom crost her threshold, yet he sent
Gifts by the children, garden-herbs and fruit,
The late and early roses from his wall,
Or conies from the down, and now and then,
With some pretext of fineness in the meal
To save the offence of charitable, flour
From his tall mill that whistled on the waste.   340

   But Philip did not fathom Annie's mind:
Scarce could the woman when he came upon her,
Out of full heart and boundless gratitude
Light on a broken word to thank him with.
But Philip was her children's all-in-all;
From distant corners of the street they ran
To greet his hearty welcome heartily;
Lords of his house and of his mill were they;
Worried his passive ear with petty wrongs
Or pleasures, hung upon him, play'd with him   350
And call'd him Father Philip. Philip gain'd
As Enoch lost; for Enoch seem'd to them

Uncertain as a vision or a dream,
Faint as a figure seen in early dawn
Down at the far end of an avenue,
Going we know not where: and so ten years,
Since Enoch left his hearth and native land,
Fled forward, and no news of Enoch came.

It chanced one evening Annie's children long'd
To go with others, nutting to the wood,   360
And Annie would go with them; then they begg'd
For Father Philip (as they call'd him) too:
Him, like the working bee in blossom-dust,
Blanch'd with his mill, they found; and saying to him
'Come with us Father Philip' he denied;
But when the children pluck'd at him to go,
He laugh'd, and yielded readily to their wish,
For was not Annie with them? and they went.

But after scaling half the weary down,
Just where the prone edge of the wood began   370
To feather toward the hollow, all her force
Fail'd her; and sighing 'let me rest' she said:
So Philip rested with her well-content;
While all the younger ones with jubilant cries
Broke from their elders, and tumultuously
Down thro' the whitening hazels made a plunge
To the bottom, and dispersed, and bent or broke
The lithe reluctant boughs to tear away
Their tawny clusters, crying to each other
And calling, here and there, about the wood.   380

But Philip sitting at her side forgot
Her presence, and remember'd one dark hour
Here in this wood, when like a wounded life
He crept into the shadow: at last he said
Lifting his honest forehead 'Listen, Annie,
How merry they are down yonder in the wood.
Tired, Annie?' for she did not speak a word.
'Tired?' but her face had fall'n upon her hands;

At which, as with a kind of anger in him,
'The ship was lost' he said 'the ship was lost!'   390
No more of that! why should you kill yourself
And make them orphans quite?' And Annie said
'I thought not of it: but – I know not why –
Their voices make me feel so solitary.'

Then Philip coming somewhat closer spoke.
'Annie, there is a thing upon my mind,
And it has been upon my mind so long,
That tho' I know not when it first came there,
I know that it will out at last. O Annie,
It is beyond all hope, against all chance,   400
That he who left you ten long years ago
Should still be living; well then – let me speak:
I grieve to see you poor and wanting help:
I cannot help you as I wish to do
Unless – they say that women are so quick –
Perhaps you know what I would have you know –
I wish you for my wife. I fain would prove
A father to your children: I do think
They love me as a father: I am sure
That I love them as if they were mine own;   410
And I believe, if you were fast my wife,
That after all these sad uncertain years,
We might be still as happy as God grants
To any of His creatures. Think upon it:
For I am well-to-do – no kin, no care,
No burthen, save my care for you and yours:
And we have known each other all our lives,
And I have loved you longer than you know.'

Then answer'd Annie; tenderly she spoke:
'You have been as God's good angel in our house.   420
God bless you for it, God reward you for it,
Philip, with something happier than myself.
Can one love twice? can you be ever loved
As Enoch was? what is it that you ask?'
'I am content' he answer'd 'to be loved

A little after Enoch.' 'O' she cried
Scared as it were 'dear Philip, wait a while:
If Enoch comes — but Enoch will not come —
Yet wait a year, a year is not so long:
Surely I shall be wiser in a year: 430
O wait a little!' Philip sadly said
'Annie, as I have waited all my life
I well may wait a little.' 'Nay' she cried
'I am bound: you have my promise — in a year:
Will you not bide your year as I bide mine?'
And Philip answer'd 'I will bide my year.'

   Here both were mute, till Philip glancing up
Beheld the dead flame of the fallen day
Pass from the Danish barrow overhead;
Then fearing night and chill for Annie rose,   440
And sent his voice beneath him thro' the wood.
Up came the children laden with their spoil;
Then all descended to the port, and there
At Annie's door he paused and gave his hand,
Saying gently 'Annie, when I spoke to you,
That was your hour of weakness. I was wrong.
I am always bound to you, but you are free.'
Then Annie weeping answer'd 'I am bound.'

   She spoke; and in one moment as it were,
While yet she went about her household ways,   450
Ev'n as she dwelt upon his latest words,
That he had loved her longer than she knew,
That autumn into autumn flash'd again,
And there he stood once more before her face,
Claiming her promise. 'Is it a year?' she ask'd.
'Yes, if the nuts' he said 'be ripe again:
Come out and see.' But she — she put him off —
So much to look to — such a change — a month —
Give her a month — she knew that she was bound —
A month — no more. Then Philip with his eyes   460
Full of that lifelong hunger, and his voice
Shaking a little like a drunkard's hand,

'Take your own time, Annie, take your own time.'
And Annie could have wept for pity of him;
And yet she held him on delayingly
With many a scarce-believable excuse,
Trying his truth and his long-sufferance,
Till half-another year had slipt away.

By this the lazy gossips of the port,
Abhorrent of a calculation crost,   470
Began to chafe as at a personal wrong.
Some thought that Philip did but trifle with her;
Some that she but held off to draw him on;
And others laugh'd at her and Philip too,
As simple folk that knew not their own minds
And one, in whom all evil fancies clung
Like serpent eggs together, laughingly
Would hint at worse in either. Her own son
Was silent, tho' he often look'd his wish;
But evermore the daughter prest upon her   480
To wed the man so dear to all of them
And lift the household out of poverty;
And Philip's rosy face contracting grew
Careworn and wan; and all these things fell on her
Sharp as reproach.

                        At last one night it chanced
That Annie could not sleep, but earnestly
Pray'd for a sign 'my Enoch is he gone?'
Then compass'd round by the blind wall of night
Brook'd not the expectant terror of her heart,
Started from bed, and struck herself a light,   490
Then desperately seized the holy Book,
Suddenly set it wide to find a sign,
Suddenly put her finger on the text,
'Under a palmtree.' That was nothing to her:
No meaning there: she closed the Book and slept:
When lo! her Enoch sitting on a height,
Under a palmtree, over him the Sun:
'He is gone' she thought 'he is happy, he is singing

153

Hosanna in the highest: yonder shines
The Sun of Righteousness, and these be palms   500
Whereof the happy people strowing cried
'"Hosanna in the highest!"' Here she woke,
Resolved, sent for him and said wildly to him
'There is no reason why we should not wed.'
'Then for God's sake,' he answer'd, 'both our sakes,
So you will wed me, let it be at once.'

  So these were wed and merrily rang the bells,
Merrily rang the bells and they were wed.
But never merrily beat Annie's heart.
A footstep seem'd to fall beside her path,   510
She knew not whence; a whisper on her ear,
She knew not what; nor loved she to be left
Alone at home, nor ventured out alone.
What ail'd her then, that ere she enter'd, often
Her hand dwelt lingeringly on the latch,
Fearing to enter: Philip thought he knew:
Such doubts and fears were common to her state,
Being with child: but when her child was born,
Then her new child was as herself renew'd,
Then the new mother came about her heart,   520
Then her good Philip was her all-in-all,
And that mysterious instinct wholly died.

  And where was Enoch? prosperously sail'd
The ship 'Good Fortune,' tho' at setting forth
The Biscay, roughly ridging eastward, shook
And almost overwhelm'd her, yet unvext
She slipt across the summer of the world,
Then after a long tumble about the Cape
And frequent interchange of foul and fair,
She passing thro' the summer world again,   530
The breath of heaven came continually
And sent her sweetly by the golden isles,
Till silent in her oriental haven.

There Enoch traded for himself, and bought
Quaint monsters for the market of those times,
A gilded dragon, also, for the babes.

Less lucky her home-voyage: at first indeed
Thro' many a fair sea-circle, day by day,
Scarce-rocking, her full-busted figure-head
Stared o'er the ripple feathering from her bows: 540
Then follow'd calms, and then winds variable,
Then baffling, a long course of them; and last
Storm, such as drove her under moonless heavens
Till hard upon the cry of 'breakers' came
The crash of ruin, and the loss of all
But Enoch and two others. Half the night,
Buoy'd upon floating tackle and broken spars,
These drifted, stranding on an isle at morn
Rich, but the loneliest in a lonely sea.

No want was there of human sustenance,   550
Soft fruitage, mighty nuts, and nourishing roots;
Nor save for pity was it hard to take
The helpless life so wild that it was tame.
There in a seaward-gazing mountain-gorge
They built, and thatch'd with leaves of palm, a hut,
Half hut, half native cavern. So the three,
Set in this Eden of all plenteousness,
Dwelt with eternal summer, ill-content.

For one, the youngest, hardly more than boy,
Hurt in that night of sudden ruin and wreck,   560
Lay lingering out a five-years' death-in-life.
They could not leave him. After he was gone,
The two remaining found a fallen stem;
And Enoch's comrade, careless of himself,
Fire-hollowing this in Indian fashion, fell
Sun-stricken, and that other lived alone.
In those two deaths he read God's warning 'wait.'

The mountain wooded to the peak, the lawns
And winding glades high up like ways to Heaven,
The slender coco's drooping crown of plumes,   570
The lightning flash of insect and of bird,
The lustre of the long convolvuluses
That coil'd around the stately stems, and ran
Ev'n to the limit of the land, the glows
And glories of the broad belt of the world,
All these he saw; but what he fain had seen
He could not see, the kindly human face,
Nor ever hear a kindly voice, but heard
The myriad shriek of wheeling ocean-fowl,
The league-long roller thundering on the reef,   580
The moving whisper of huge trees that branch'd
And blossom'd in the zenith, or the sweep
Of some precipitous rivulet to the wave,
As down the shore he ranged, or all day long
Sat often in the seaward-gazing gorge,
A shipwreck'd sailor, waiting for a sail:
No sail from day to day, but every day
The sunrise broken into scarlet shafts
Among the palms and ferns and precipices;
The blaze upon the waters to the east;   590
The blaze upon his island overhead;
The blaze upon the waters to the west;
Then the great stars that globed themselves in Heaven,
The hollower-bellowing ocean, and again
The scarlet shafts of sunrise – but no sail.

There often as he watch'd or seem'd to watch,
So still, the golden lizard on him paused,
A phantom made of many phantoms moved
Before him haunting him, or he himself
Moved haunting people, things and places, known   600
Far in a darker isle beyond the line;
The babes, their babble, Annie, the small house,
The climbing street, the mill, the leafy lanes,
The peacock-yewtree and the lonely Hall,
The horse he drove, the boat he sold, the chill

November dawns and dewy-glooming downs,
The gentle shower, the smell of dying leaves,
And the low moan of leaden-colour'd seas.

  Once likewise, in the ringing of his ears,
Tho' faintly, merrily – far and far away –   610
He heard the pealing of his parish bells;
Then, tho' he knew not wherefore, started up
Shuddering, and when the beauteous hateful isle
Return'd upon him, had not his poor heart
Spoken with That, which being everywhere
Lets none, who speaks with Him, seem all alone,
Surely the man had died of solitude.

  Thus over Enoch's early-silvering head
The sunny and rainy seasons came and went
Year after year. His hopes to see his own,   620
And pace the sacred old familiar fields,
Not yet had perish'd, when his lonely doom
Came suddenly to an end. Another ship
(She wanted water) blown by baffling winds,
Like the Good Fortune, from her destined course,
Stay'd by this isle, not knowing where she lay:
For since the mate had seen at early dawn
Across a break on the mist-wreathen isle
The silent water slipping from the hills,
They sent a crew that landing burst away   630
In search of stream or fount, and fill'd the shores
With clamour. Downward from his mountain gorge
Stept the long-hair'd long-bearded solitary,
Brown, looking hardly human, strangely clad,
Muttering and mumbling, idiotlike it seem'd,
With inarticulate rage, and making signs
They knew not what: and yet he led the way
To where the rivulets of sweet water ran;
And ever as he mingled with the crew,
And heard them talking, his long-bounden tongue   640
Was loosen'd, till he made them understand;
Whom, when their casks were fill'd they took aboard:

157

And there the tale he utter'd brokenly,
Scarce credited at first but more and more,
Amazed and melted all who listen'd to it:
And clothes they gave him and free passage home
But oft he work'd among the rest and shook
His isolation from him. None of these
Came from his country, or could answer him,
If question'd, aught of what he cared to know.   650
And dull the voyage was with long delays,
The vessel scarce sea-worthy; but evermore
His fancy fled before the lazy wind
Returning, till beneath a clouded moon
He like a lover down thro' all his blood
Drew in the dewy meadowy morning-breath
Of England, blown across her ghostly wall:
And that same morning officers and men
Levied a kindly tax upon themselves,
Pitying the lonely man, and gave him it: 660
Then moving up the coast they landed him,
Ev'n in that harbour whence he sail'd before.

    There Enoch spoke no word to anyone,
But homeward – home – what home? had he a home?
His home, he walk'd. Bright was that afternoon,
Sunny but chill; till drawn thro' either chasm,
Where either haven open'd on the deeps,
Roll'd a sea-haze and whelm'd the world in gray;
Cut off the length of highway on before,
And left but narrow breadth to left and right   670
Of wither'd holt or tilth or pasturage.
On the nigh-naked tree the robin piped
Disconsolate, and thro' the dripping haze
The dead weight of the dead leaf bore it down:
Thicker the drizzle grew, deeper the gloom;
Last, as it seem'd, a great mist-blotted light
Flared on him, and he came upon the place.

    Then down the long street having slowly stolen,
His heart foreshadowing all calamity,

His eyes upon the stones, he reach'd the home
Where Annie lived and loved him, and his babes
In those far-off seven happy years were born;
But finding neither light nor murmur there
(A bill of sale gleam'd thro' the drizzle) crept
Still downward thinking 'dead or dead to me!'

Down to the pool and narrow wharf he went,
Seeking a tavern which of old he knew,
A front of timber-crost antiquity,
So propt, worm-eaten, ruinously old,
He thought it must have gone; but he was gone
Who kept it; and his widow, Miriam Lane,
With daily-dwindling profits held the house;
A haunt of brawling seamen once, but now
Stiller, with yet a bed for wandering men.
There Enoch rested silent many days.

But Miriam Lane was good and garrulous,
Nor let him be, but often breaking in,
Told him, with other annals of the port,
Not knowing – Enoch was so brown, so bow'd,
So broken – all the story of his house.
His baby's death, her growing poverty,
How Philip put her little ones to school,
And kept them in it, his long wooing her,
Her slow consent, and marriage, and the birth
Of Philip's child: and o'er his countenance
No shadow past, nor motion: anyone,
Regarding, well had deem'd he felt the tale
Less than the teller: only when she closed
'Enoch, poor man, was cast away and lost'
He, shaking his gray head pathetically,
Repeated muttering 'cast away and lost;'
Again in deeper inward whispers 'lost!'

But Enoch yearn'd to see her face again;
'If I might look on her sweet face again
And know that she is happy.' So the thought

690

700

710

159

Haunted and harass'd him, and drove him forth,
At evening when the dull November day
Was growing duller twilight, to the hill.
There he sat down gazing on all below;
There did a thousand memories roll upon him,   720
Unspeakable for sadness. By and by
The ruddy square of comfortable light,
Far-blazing from the rear of Philip's house,
Allured him, as the beacon-blaze allures
The bird of passage, till he madly strikes
Against it, and beats out his weary life.

For Philip's dwelling fronted on the street,
The latest house to landward; but behind,
With one small gate that open'd on the waste,
Flourish'd a little garden square and wall'd: 730
And in it throve an ancient evergreen,
A yewtree, and all round it ran a walk
Of shingle, and a walk divided it:
But Enoch shunn'd the middle walk and stole
Up by the wall, behind the yew; and thence
That which he better might have shunn'd, if griefs
Like his have worse or better, Enoch saw.

For cups and silver on the burnish'd board
Sparkled and shone; so genial was the hearth:
And on the right hand of the hearth he saw   740
Philip, the slighted suitor of old times,
Stout, rosy, with his babe across his knees;
And o'er her second father stoopt a girl,
A later but a loftier Annie Lee,
Fair-hair'd and tall, and from her lifted hand
Dangled a length of ribbon and a ring
To tempt the babe, who rear'd his creasy arms,
Caught at and ever miss'd it, and they laugh'd:
And on the left hand of the hearth he saw
The mother glancing often toward her babe,   750
But turning now and then to speak with him,
Her son, who stood beside her tall and strong,
And saying that which pleased him, for he smiled.

160

Now when the dead man come to life beheld
His wife his wife no more, and saw the babe
Hers, yet not his, upon the father's knee,
And all the warmth, the peace, the happiness,
And his own children tall and beautiful,
And him, that other, reigning in his place,
Lord of his rights and of his children's love, –   760
Then he, tho' Miriam Lane had told him all,
Because things seen are mightier than things heard,
Stagger'd and shook, holding the branch, and fear'd
To send abroad a shrill and terrible cry,
Which in one moment, like the blast of doom,
Would shatter all the happiness of the hearth.

He therefore turning softly like a thief,
Lest the harsh shingle should grate underfoot,
And feeling all along the garden-wall,
Lest he should swoon and tumble and be found,   770
Crept to the gate, and open'd it, and closed,
As lightly as a sick man's chamber-door,
Behind him, and came out upon the waste.

And there he would have knelt, but that his knees
Were feeble, so that falling prone he dug
His fingers into the wet earth, and pray'd.

'Too hard to bear! why did they take me thence?
O God Almighty, blessed Saviour, Thou
That did'st uphold me on my lonely isle,
Uphold me, Father, in my loneliness   780
A little longer! aid me, give me strength
Not to tell her, never to let her know.
Help me not to break in upon her peace.
My children too! must I not speak to these?
They know me not. I should betray myself.
Never: no father's kiss for me – the girl
So like her mother, and the boy, my son.'

There speech and thought and nature fail'd a little,
And he lay tranced; but when he rose and paced
Back toward his solitary home again,   790
All down the long and narrow street he went
Beating it in upon his weary brain,
As tho' it were the burthen of a song,
'Not to tell her, never to let her know.'

He was not all unhappy. His resolve
Upbore him, and firm faith, and evermore
Prayer from a living source within the will,
And beating up thro' all the bitter world,
Like fountains of sweet water in the sea,
Kept him a living soul. 'This miller's wife'   800
He said to Miriam 'that you spoke about,
Has she no fear that her first husband lives?'
'Ay, ay, poor soul' said Miriam, 'fear enow!
If you could tell her you had seen him dead,
Why, that would be her comfort;' and he thought
'After the Lord has call'd me she shall know,
I wait His time' and Enoch set himself,
Scorning an alms, to work whereby to live.
Almost to all things could he turn his hand.
Cooper he was and carpenter, and wrought   810
To make the boatmen fishing-nets, or help'd
At lading and unlading the tall barks,
That brought the stinted commerce of those days;
Thus earn'd a scanty living for himself:
Yet since he did but labour for himself,
Work without hope, there was not life in it
Whereby the man could live; and as the year
Roll'd itself round again to meet the day
When Enoch had return'd, a languor came
Upon him, gentle sickness, gradually   820
Weakening the man, till he could do no more,
But kept the house, his chair, and last his bed.
And Enoch bore his weakness cheerfully.
For sure no gladlier does the stranded wreck
See thro' the gray skirts of a lifting squall

The boat that bears the hope of life approach
To save the life despair'd of, than he saw
Death dawning on him, and the close of all.

For thro' that dawning gleam'd a kindlier hope
On Enoch thinking 'after I am gone,   830
Then may she learn I loved her to the last.'
He call'd aloud for Miriam Lane and said
'Woman, I have a secret — only swear,
Before I tell you — swear upon the book
Not to reveal it, till you see me dead.'
'Dead' clamour'd the good woman 'hear him talk!
I warrant, man, that we shall bring you round.'
'Swear' added Enoch sternly 'on the book.'
And on the book, half-frighted, Miriam swore.
Then Enoch rolling his gray eyes upon her,   840
'Did you know Enoch Arden of this town?'
'Know him?' she said 'I knew him far away.
Ay, ay, I mind him coming down the street;
Held his head high, and cared for no man, he.'
Slowly and sadly Enoch answer'd her;
'His head is low, and no man cares for him.
I think I have not three days more to live;
I am the man.' At which the woman gave
A half-incredulous, half-hysterical cry.
'You Arden, you! nay, — sure he was a foot   850
Higher than you be.' Enoch said again
'My God has bow'd me down to what I am;
My grief and solitude have broken me;
Nevertheless, know you that I am he
Who married — but that name has twice been changed —
I married her who married Philip Ray.
Sit, listen.' Then he told her of his voyage,
His wreck, his lonely life, his coming back,
His gazing in on Annie, his resolve,
And how he kept it. As the woman heard,   860
Fast flow'd the current of her easy tears,
While in her heart she yearn'd incessantly
To rush abroad all round the little haven,

Proclaiming Enoch Arden and his woes;
But awed and promise-bounden she forbore,
Saying only 'See your bairns before you go!
Eh, let me fetch 'em, Arden,' and arose
Eager to bring them down, for Enoch hung
A moment on her words, but then replied.

'Woman, disturb me not now at the last,   870
But let me hold my purpose till I die.
Sit down again; mark me and understand,
While I have power to speak. I charge you now,
When you shall see her, tell her that I died
Blessing her, praying for her, loving her;
Save for the bar between us, loving her
As when she laid her head beside my own.
And tell my daughter Annie, whom I saw
So like her mother, that my latest breath
Was spent in blessing her and praying for her.   880
And tell my son that I died blessing him.
And say to Philip that I blest him too;
He never meant us any thing but good.
But if my children care to see me dead,
Who hardly knew me living, let them come,
I am their father; but she must not come,
For my dead face would vex her after-life.
And now there is but one of all my blood,
Who will embrace me in the world-to-be:
This hair is his: she cut it off and gave it,   890
And I have borne it with me all these years,
And thought to bear it with me to my grave;
But now my mind is changed, for I shall see him,
My babe in bliss: wherefore when I am gone,
Take, give her this, for it may comfort her:
It will moreover be a token to her,
That I am he.'

              He ceased; and Miriam Lane
Made such a voluble answer promising all,
That once again he roll'd his eyes upon her

Repeating all he wish'd, and once again   900
She promised.

                    Then the third night after this,
While Enoch slumber'd motionless and pale,
And Miriam watch'd and dozed at intervals,
There came so loud a calling of the sea,
That all the houses in the haven rang.
He woke, he rose, he spread his arms abroad
Crying with a loud voice 'a sail! a sail!
I am saved'; and so fell back and spoke no more.

  So past the strong heroic soul away.
And when they buried him the little port   910
Had seldom seen a costlier funeral.

FLOWER IN THE CRANNIED WALL

Flower in the crannied wall,
I pluck you out of the crannies,
I hold you here, root and all, in my hand,
Little flower – but *if* I could understand
What you are, root and all, and all in all,
I should know what God and man is.

RIZPAH

I

Wailing, wailing, wailing, the wind over land and sea –
And Willy's voice in the wind, 'O mother, come out to me.'
Why should he call me tonight, when he knows that I
          cannot go?
For the downs are as bright as day, and the full moon stares at
          the snow.

165

II

We should be seen, my dear; they would spy us out of the
town.
The loud black nights for us, and the storm rushing over the
down,
When I cannot see my own hand, but am led by the creak of
the chain,
And grovel and grope for my son till I find myself drenched
with the rain.

III

Anything fallen again? nay – what was there left to fall?
I have taken them home, I have numbered the bones, I have
hidden them all.   10
What am I saying? and what are *you*? do you come as a spy?
Falls? what falls? who knows? As the tree falls so must it lie.

IV

Who let her in? how long has she been? you – what have you
heard?
Why did you sit so quiet? you never have spoken a word.
O – to pray with me – yes – a lady – none of their spies –
But the night has crept into my heart, and begun to darken
my eyes.

V

Ah – you, that have lived so soft, what should *you* know of
the night,
The blast and the burning shame and the bitter frost and the
fright?
I have done it, while you were asleep – you were only made
for the day.
I have gathered my baby together – and now you may go
your way.   20

VI

Nay – for it's kind of you, Madam, to sit by an old dying wife.
But say nothing hard of my boy, I have only an hour of life.

166

I kissed my boy in the prison, before he went out to die.
'They dared me to do it,' he said, and he never has told me
    a lie.
I whipt him for robbing an orchard once when he was but
    a child –
'The farmer dared me to do it,' he said; he was always so
    wild –
And idle – and couldn't be idle – my Willy – he never could
    rest.
The King should have made him a soldier, he would have been
    one of his best.

VII

But he lived with a lot of wild mates, and they never would
    let him be good;
They swore that he dare not rob the mail, and he swore that
    he would;   30
And he took no life, but he took one purse, and when all was
    done
He flung it among his fellows – I'll none of it, said my son.

VIII

I came into court to the Judge and the lawyers. I told them
    my tale,
God's own truth – but they killed him, they killed him for
    robbing the mail.
They hanged him in chains for a show – we had always borne
    a good name –
To be hanged for a thief – and then put away – isn't that
    enough shame?
Dust to dust – low down – let us hide! but they set him
    so high
That all the ships of the world could stare at him, passing by.
God 'ill pardon the hell-black raven and horrible fowls of
    the air,
But not the black heart of the lawyer who killed him and
    hanged him there.   40

167

IX

And the jailer forced me away. I had bid him my last goodbye;
They had fastened the door of his cell. 'O mother!' I heard
    him cry.
I couldn't get back though I tried, he had something further
    to say,
And now I never shall know it. The jailer forced me away.

X

Then since I couldn't but hear that cry of my boy that was
    dead,
They seized me and shut me up: they fastened me down on
    my bed.
'Mother, O mother!' – he called in the dark to me year
    after year –
They beat me for that, they beat me – you know that I
    couldn't but hear;
And then at the last they found I had grown so stupid and
    still
They let me abroad again – but the creatures had worked
    their will.   50

XI

Flesh of my flesh was gone, but bone of my bone was left –
I stole them all from the lawyers – and you, will you call it
    a theft? –
My baby, the bones that had sucked me, the bones that had
    laughed and had cried –
Theirs? O no! they are mine – not theirs – they had moved
    in my side.

XII

Do you think I was scared by the bones? I kissed 'em, I buried
    'em all –
I can't dig deep, I am old – in the night by the churchyard
    wall.
My Willy 'ill rise up whole when the trumpet of judgment
    'ill sound,
But I charge you never to say that I laid him in holy ground.

XIII

They would scratch him up – they would hang him again
        on the cursèd tree.
Sin? O yes – we are sinners, I know – let all that be,   60
And read me a Bible verse of the Lord's good will toward
        men –
'Full of compassion and mercy, the Lord' – let me hear it
        again;
'Full of compassion and mercy – long-suffering.' Yes, O yes!
For the lawyer is born but to murder – the Saviour lives but
        to bless.
He'll never put on the black cap except for the worst of the
        worst,
And the first may be last – I have heard it in church – and
        the last may be first.
Suffering – O long-suffering – yes, as the Lord must know,
Year after year in the mist and the wind and the shower and
        the snow.

XIV

Heard, have you? what? they have told you he never repented
        his sin.
How do they know it? are *they* his mother? are *you* of his
        kin?   70
Heard! have you ever heard, when the storm on the downs
        began,
The wind that 'ill wail like a child and the sea that 'ill moan
        like a man?

XV

Election, Election and Reprobation – it's all very well.
But I go tonight to my boy, and I shall not find him in Hell.
For I cared so much for my boy that the Lord has looked
        into my care,
And He means me I'm sure to be happy with Willy, I know
        not where.

XVI

And if *he* be lost – but to save *my* soul that is all your desire:
Do you think that I care for *my* soul if my boy be gone to
    the fire?
I have been with God in the dark – go, go, you may leave
    me alone –
You never have borne a child – you are just as hard as
    a stone.   80

XVII

Madam, I beg your pardon! I think that you mean to be kind,
But I cannot hear what you say for my Willy's voice in the
    wind –
The snow and the sky so bright – he used but to call in the
    dark,
And he calls to me now from the church and not from the
    gibbet – for hark!
Nay – you can hear it yourself – it is coming – shaking the
    walls –
Willy – the moon's in a cloud – Good-night. I am going.
    He calls.

IN THE CHILDREN'S HOSPITAL

I

Our doctor had called in another, I never had seen him before,
But he sent a chill to my heart when I saw him come in at the
    door,
Fresh from the surgery-schools of France and of other lands –
Harsh red hair, big voice, big chest, big merciless hands!
Wonderful cures he had done, O yes, but they said too of
    him
He was happier using the knife than in trying to save the
    limb,
And that I can well believe, for he looked so coarse and
    so red,
I could think he was one of those who would break their jests
    on the dead,

And mangle the living dog that had loved him and fawned at
      his knee –
Drenched with the hellish oorali – that ever such things should
      be!   10

II

Here was a boy – I am sure that some of our children
      would die
But for the voice of Love, and the smile, and the comforting
      eye –
Here was a boy in the ward, every bone seemed out of its
      place –
Caught in a mill and crushed – it was all but a hopeless case:
And he handled him gently enough; but his voice and his
      face were not kind,
And it was but a hopeless case, he had seen it and made up
      his mind,
And he said to me roughly 'The lad will need little more of
      your care.'
'All the more need,' I told him, 'to seek the Lord Jesus in
      prayer;
They are all his children here, and I pray for them all as my
      own:'
But he turned to me, 'Ay, good woman, can prayer set a
      broken bone?'   20
Then he muttered half to himself, but I know that I heard
      him say
'All very well – but the good Lord Jesus has had his day.'

III

Had? has it come? It has only dawned. It will come by
      and by.
O how could I serve in the wards if the hope of the world
      were a lie?
How could I bear with the sights and the loathsome smells
      of disease
But that He said 'Ye do it to me, when ye do it to these'?

IV

So he went. And we past to this ward where the younger
    children are laid:
Here is the cot of our orphan, our darling, our meek little
    maid;
Empty you see just now! We have lost her who loved her so
    much –
Patient of pain though as quick as a sensitive plant to the
    touch;   30
Hers was the prettiest prattle, it often moved me to tears,
Hers was the gratefullest heart I have found in a child of her
    years –
Nay you remember our Emmie; you used to send her the
    flowers;
How she would smile at 'em, play with 'em, talk to 'em
    hours after hours!
They that can wander at will where the works of the Lord are
    revealed
Little guess what joy can be got from a cowslip out of the
    field;
Flowers to these 'spirits in prison' are all they can know of the
    spring,
They freshen and sweeten the wards like the waft of an Angel's
    wing;
And she lay with a flower in one hand and her thin hands
    crost on her breast –
Wan, but as pretty as heart can desire, and we thought her
    at rest,   40
Quietly sleeping – so quiet, our doctor said 'Poor little dear,
Nurse, I must do it tomorrow; she'll never live through it,
    I fear.'

V

I walked with our kindly old doctor as far as the head of the
    stair,
Then I returned to the ward; the child didn't see I was there.

VI

Never since I was nurse, had I been so grieved and so vext!
Emmie had heard him. Softly she called from her cot to the
    next,
'He says I shall never live through it, O Annie, what shall
    I do?'
Annie considered. 'If I,' said the wise little Annie, 'was you,
I should cry to the dear Lord Jesus to help me, for, Emmie,
    you see,
It's all in the picture there: "Little children should come
    to me."'   50
(Meaning the print that you gave us, I find that it always can
    please
Our children, the dear Lord Jesus with children about his
    knees.)
'Yes, and I will,' said Emmie, 'but then if I call to the Lord,
How should he know that it's me? such a lot of beds in the
    ward!'
That was a puzzle for Annie. Again she considered and said:
'Emmie, you put out your arms, and you leave 'em outside on
    the bed –
The Lord has so *much* to see to! but, Emmie, you tell it him
    plain,
It's the little girl with her arms lying out on the counterpane.'

VII

I had sat three nights by the child – I could not watch her
    for four –
My brain had begun to reel – I felt I could do it no more.   60
That was my sleeping-night, but I thought that it never would
    pass.
There was a thunderclap once, and a clatter of hail on the
    glass,
And there was a phantom cry that I heard as I tost about,
The motherless bleat of a lamb in the storm and the darkness
    without;
My sleep was broken besides with dreams of the dreadful knife
And fears for our delicate Emmie who scarce would escape
    with her life;

Then in the gray of the morning it seemed she stood by me
    and smiled,
And the doctor came at his hour, and we went to see to the
    child.

VIII

He had brought his ghastly tools: we believed her asleep
    again –
Her dear, long, lean, little arms lying out on the counterpane;
Say that His day is done! Ah why should we care what they
    say?   70
The Lord of the children had heard her, and Emmie had past
    away.

THE SISTERS

They have left the doors ajar; and by their clash,
And prelude on the keys, I know the song,
Their favourite – which I call 'The Tables Turned.'
Evelyn begins it 'O diviner Air.'

Evelyn

O diviner Air,
Through the heat, the drowth, the dust, the glare,
Far from out the west in shadowing showers,
Over all the meadow baked and bare,
Making fresh and fair
All the bowers and the flowers,   10
Fainting flowers, faded bowers,
Over all this weary world of ours,
Breathe, diviner Air!

A sweet voice that – you scarce could better that.
Now follows Edith echoing Evelyn.

Edith

O diviner light,
Through the cloud that roofs our noon with night,
Through the blotting mist, the blinding showers,

174

Far from out a sky for ever bright,
Over all the woodland's flooded bowers,   20
Over all the meadow's drowning flowers,
Over all this ruined world of ours,
Break, diviner light!

Marvellously like, their voices — and themselves!
Though one is somewhat deeper than the other,
As one is somewhat graver than the other —
Edith than Evelyn. Your good Uncle, whom
You count the father of your fortune, longs
For this alliance: let me ask you then,
Which voice most takes you? for I do not doubt   30
Being a watchful parent, you are taken
With one or other: though sometimes I fear
You may be flickering, fluttering in a doubt
Between the two — which must not be — which might
Be death to one: they both are beautiful:
Evelyn is gayer, wittier, prettier, says
The common voice, if one may trust it: she?
No! but the paler and the graver, Edith.
Woo her and gain her then: no wavering, boy!
The graver is perhaps the one for you   40
Who jest and laugh so easily and so well.
For love will go by contrast, as by likes.

    No sisters ever prized each other more.
Not so: their mother and her sister loved
More passionately still.
                    But that my best
And oldest friend, your Uncle, wishes it,
And that I know you worthy everyway
To be my son, I might, perchance, be loath
To part them, or part from them: and yet one
Should marry, or all the broad lands in your view   50
From this bay window — which our house has held
Three hundred years — will pass collaterally.

My father with a child on either knee,
A hand upon the head of either child,
Smoothing their locks, as golden as his own
Were silver, 'get them wedded' would he say.
And once my prattling Edith asked him 'why?'
Ay, why? said he, 'for why should I go lame?'
Then told them of his wars, and of his wound.
For see – this wine – the grape from whence it flowed   60
Was blackening on the slopes of Portugal,
When that brave soldier, down the terrible ridge
Plunged in the last fierce charge at Waterloo,
And caught the laming bullet. He left me this,
Which yet retains a memory of its youth,
As I of mine, and my first passion. Come!
Here's to your happy union with my child!

Yet must you change your name: no fault of mine!
You say that you can do it as willingly
As birds make ready for their bridal-time   70
By change of feather: for all that, my boy,
Some birds are sick and sullen when they moult.
An old and worthy name! but mine that stirred
Among our civil wars and earlier too
Among the Roses, the more venerable.
I care not for a name – no fault of mine.
Once more – a happier marriage than my own!

You see yon Lombard poplar on the plain.
The highway running by it leaves a breadth
Of sward to left and right, where, long ago,   80
One bright May morning in a world of song,
I lay at leisure, watching overhead
The aërial poplar wave, an amber spire.

I dozed; I woke. An open landaulet
Whirled by, which, after it had past me, showed
Turning my way, the loveliest face on earth.
The face of one there sitting opposite,
On whom I brought a strange unhappiness,

That time I did not see.
                              Love at first sight
May seem – with goodly rhyme and reason for it –   90
Possible – at first glimpse, and for a face
Gone in a moment – strange. Yet once, when first
I came on lake Llanberris in the dark,
A moonless night with storm – one lightning-fork
Flashed out the lake; and though I loitered there
The full day after, yet in retrospect
That less than momentary thunder-sketch
Of lake and mountain conquers all the day.

  The sun himself has limned the face for me.
Not quite so quickly, no, nor half as well.   100
For look you here – the shadows are too deep,
And like the critic's blurring comment make
The veriest beauties of the work appear
The darkest faults: the sweet eyes frown: the lips
Seem but a gash. My sole memorial
Of Edith – no, the other, – both indeed.

  So that bright face was flashed through sense and soul
And by the poplar vanished – to be found
Long after, as it seemed, beneath the tall
Tree-bowers, and those long-sweeping beechen boughs   110
Of our New Forest. I was there alone:
The phantom of the whirling landaulet
For ever past me by: when one quick peal
Of laughter drew me through the glimmering glades
Down to the snowlike sparkle of a cloth
On fern and foxglove. Lo, the face again,
My Rosalind in this Arden – Edith – all
One bloom of youth, health, beauty, happiness,
And moved to merriment at a passing jest.

  There one of those about her knowing me   120
Called me to join them; so with these I spent
What seemed my crowning hour, my day of days.

177

I wooed her then, nor unsuccessfully,
The worse for her, for me! was I content?
Ay – no, not quite; for now and then I thought
Laziness, vague love-longings, the bright May,
Had made a heated haze to magnify
The charm of Edith – that a man's ideal
Is high in Heaven, and lodged with Plato's God,
Not findable here – content, and not content,   130
In some such fashion as a man may be
That having had the portrait of his friend
Drawn by an artist, looks at it, and says,
'Good! very like! not altogether he.'

As yet I had not bound myself by words,
Only, believing I loved Edith, made
Edith love *me*. Then came the day when I,
Flattering myself that all my doubts were fools
Born of the fool this Age that doubts of all –
Not I that day of Edith's love or mine –   140
Had braced my purpose to declare myself:
I stood upon the stairs of Paradise.
The golden gates would open at a word.
I spoke it – told her of my passion, seen
And lost and found again, had got so far,
Had caught her hand, her eyelids fell – I heard
Wheels, and a noise of welcome at the doors –
On a sudden after two Italian years
Had set the blossom of her health again,
The younger sister, Evelyn, entered – there,   150
There was the face, and altogether she.
The mother fell about the daughter's neck,
The sisters closed in one another's arms,
Their people thronged about them from the hall,
And in the thick of question and reply
I fled the house, driven by one angel face,
And all the Furies.
                        I was bound to her;
I could not free myself in honour – bound
Not by the sounded letter of the word,

But counterpressures of the yielded hand   160
That timorously and faintly echoed mine,
Quick blushes, the sweet dwelling of her eyes
Upon me when she thought I did not see –
Were these not bonds? nay, nay, but could I wed her
Loving the other? do her that great wrong?
Had I not dreamed I loved her yestermorn?
Had I not known where Love, at first a fear,
Grew after marriage to full height and form?
Yet after marriage, that mock-sister there –
Brother-in-law – the fiery nearness of it –   170
Unlawful and disloyal brotherhood –
What end but darkness could ensue from this
For all the three? So Love and Honour jarred
Though Love and Honour joined to raise the full
High-tide of doubt that swayed me up and down
Advancing nor retreating.
                    Edith wrote:
'My mother bids me ask' (I did not tell you –
A widow with less guile than many a child.
God help the wrinkled children that are Christ's
As well as the plump cheek – she wrought us harm,   180
Poor soul, not knowing) 'are you ill?' (so ran
The letter) 'you have not been here of late.
You will not find me here. At last I go
On that long-promised visit to the North.
I told your wayside story to my mother
And Evelyn. She remembers you. Farewell.
Pray come and see my mother. Almost blind
With ever-growing cataract, yet she thinks
She sees you when she hears. Again farewell.'

    Cold words from one I had hoped to warm so far   190
That I could stamp my image on her heart!
'Pray come and see my mother, and farewell.'
Cold, but as welcome as free airs of heaven
After a dungeon's closeness. Selfish, strange!
What dwarfs are men! my strangled vanity
Uttered a stifled cry – to have vext myself

And all in vain for her − cold heart or none −
No bride for me. Yet so my path was clear
To win the sister.

                Whom I wooed and won.
  For Evelyn knew not of my former suit,   200
Because the simple mother worked upon
By Edith prayed me not to whisper of it.
And Edith would be bridesmaid on the day.

  But on that day, not being all at ease,
I from the altar glancing back upon her,
Before the first 'I will' was uttered, saw
The bridesmaid pale, statuelike, passionless −
'No harm, no harm' I turned again, and placed
My ring upon the finger of my bride.

  So, when we parted, Edith spoke no word,   210
She wept no tear, but round my Evelyn clung
In utter silence for so long, I thought
'What, will she never set her sister free?'

  We left her, happy each in each, and then,
As though the happiness of each in each
Were not enough, must fain have torrents, lakes,
Hills, the great things of Nature and the fair,
To lift us as it were from commonplace,
And help us to our joy. Better have sent
Our Edith through the glories of the earth,   220
To change with her horizon, if true Love
Were not his own imperial all-in-all.

  Far off we went. My God, I would not live
Save that I think this gross hard-seeming world
Is our misshaping vision of the Powers
Behind the world, that make our griefs our gains.

  For on the dark night of our marriage-day
The great Tragedian, that had quenched herself
In that assumption of the bridesmaid − she
That loved me − our true Edith − her brain broke   230

With over-acting, till she rose and fled
Beneath a pitiless rush of Autumn rain
To the deaf church — to be let in — to pray
Before *that* altar — so I think; and there
They found her beating the hard Protestant doors.
She died and she was buried ere we knew.

I learnt it first. I had to speak. At once
The bright quick smile of Evelyn, that had sunned
The morning of our marriage, past away:
And on our home-return the daily want   240
Of Edith in the house, the garden, still
Haunted us like her ghost; and by and by,
Either from that necessity for talk
Which lives with blindness, or plain innocence
Of nature, or desire that her lost child
Should earn from both the praise of heroism,
The mother broke her promise to the dead,
And told the living daughter with what love
Edith had welcomed my brief wooing of her,
And all her sweet self-sacrifice and death.   250

Henceforth that mystic bond betwixt the twins —
Did I not tell you they were twins? — prevailed
So far that no caress could win my wife
Back to that passionate answer of full heart
I had from her at first. Not that her love,
Though scarce as great as Edith's power of love,
Had lessened, but the mother's garrulous wail
For ever woke the unhappy Past again,
Till that dead bridesmaid, meant to be my bride,
Put forth cold hands between us, and I feared   260
The very fountains of her life were chilled;
So took her thence, and brought her here, and here
She bore a child, whom reverently we called
Edith; and in the second year was born
A second — this I named from her own self,
Evelyn; then two weeks — no more — she joined,
In and beyond the grave, that one she loved.

Now in this quiet of declining life,
Through dreams by night and trances of the day,
The sisters glide about me hand in hand, 270
Both beautiful alike, nor can I tell
One from the other, no, nor care to tell
One from the other, only know they come,
They smile upon me, till, remembering all
The love they both have borne me, and the love
I bore them both – divided as I am
From either by the stillness of the grave –
I know not which of these I love the best.

But *you* love Edith; and her own true eyes
Are traitors to her; our quick Evelyn – 280
The merrier, prettier, wittier, as they talk,
And not without good reason, my good son –
Is yet untouched: and I, that hold them both
Dearest of all things – well, I am not sure –
But if there lie a preference eitherway,
And in the rich vocabulary of Love
'Most dearest' be a true superlative –
I think *I* likewise love your Edith most.

IN THE GARDEN AT SWAINSTON

Nightingales warbled without,
    Within was weeping for thee:
Shadows of three dead men
    Walk'd in the walks with me,
    Shadows of three dead men and thou wast one of the three.

Nightingales sang in his woods:
    The Master was far away;
Nightingales warbled and sang
    Of a passion that lasts but a day;
    Still in the house in his coffin the Prince of courtesy lay. 10

182

Two dead men have I known
   In courtesy like to thee:
Two dead men have I loved
   With a love that ever will be:
   Three dead men have I loved and thou art last of the three.

TO THE REV. W. H. BROOKFIELD

Brooks, for they called you so that knew you best,
Old Brooks, who loved so well to mouth my rhymes,
How oft we two have heard St Mary's chimes!
How oft the Cantab supper, host and guest,
Would echo helpless laughter to your jest!
How oft with him we paced that walk of limes,
Him, the lost light of those dawn-golden times,
Who loved you well! Now both are gone to rest.
You man of humorous-melancholy mark,
Dead of some inward agony – is it so?   10
Our kindlier, trustier Jacques, past away!
I cannot laud this life, it looks so dark:
Σκιᾶς ὄναρ – dream of a shadow, go –
God bless you. I shall join you in a day.

TO E. FITZGERALD

Old Fitz, who from your suburb grange,
   Where once I tarried for a while,
Glance at the wheeling Orb of change,
   And greet it with a kindly smile;
Whom yet I see as there you sit
   Beneath your sheltering garden-tree,
And watch your doves about you flit,
   And plant on shoulder, hand and knee,
Or on your head their rosy feet,
   As if they knew your diet spares   10
Whatever moved in that full sheet
   Let down to Peter at his prayers;

Who live on milk and meal and grass;
   And once for ten long weeks I tried
Your table of Pythagoras,
   And seem'd at first 'a thing enskied'
(As Shakespeare has it) airy-light
   To float above the ways of men,
Then fell from that half-spiritual height
   Chill'd, till I tasted flesh again   20
One night when earth was winter-black,
   And all the heavens flash'd in frost;
And on me, half-asleep, came back
   That wholesome heat the blood had lost,
And set me climbing icy capes
   And glaciers, over which there roll'd
To meet me long-arm'd vines with grapes
   Of Eshcol hugeness; for the cold
Without, and warmth within me, wrought
   To mould the dream; but none can say   30
That Lenten fare makes Lenten thought,
   Who reads your golden Eastern lay,
Than which I know no version done
   In English more divinely well;
A planet equal to the sun
   Which cast it, that large infidel
Your Omar; and your Omar drew
   Full-handed plaudits from our best
In modern letters, and from two,
   Old friends outvaluing all the rest,   40
Two voices heard on earth no more;
   But we old friends are still alive,
And I am nearing seventy-four,
   While you have touch'd at seventy-five,
And so I send a birthday line
   Of greeting; and my son, who dipt
In some forgotten book of mine
   With sallow scraps of manuscript,
And dating many a year ago,
   Has hit on this, which you will take   50
My Fitz, and welcome, as I know

Less for its own than for the sake
Of one recalling gracious times,
  When, in our younger London days,
You found some merit in my rhymes,
  And I more pleasure in your praise.

TO MARY BOYLE

I

'Spring-flowers'! While you still delay to take
    Your leave of town,
Our elm-tree's ruddy-hearted blossom-flake
  Is fluttering down.

II

Be truer to your promise. There! I heard
    Our cuckoo call.
Be needle to the magnet of your word,
    Not wait, till all

III

Our vernal bloom from every vale and plain
    And garden pass,   10
And all the gold from each laburnum chain
    Drop to the grass.

IV

Is memory with your Marian gone to rest,
    Dead with the dead?
For ere she left us, when we met, you prest
    My hand, and said

V

'I come with your spring-flowers.' You came not, friend;
    My birds would sing,
You heard not. Take then this spring-flower I send,
    This song of spring,   20

185

VI

Found yesterday – forgotten mine own rhyme
    By mine old self,
As I shall be forgotten by old Time,
    Laid on the shelf –

VII

A rhyme that flower'd betwixt the whitening sloe
    And kingcup blaze,
And more than half a hundred years ago,
    In rick-fire days,

VIII

When Dives loathed the times, and paced his land
    In fear of worse,
And sanguine Lazarus felt a vacant hand
    Fill with *his* purse.

30

IX

For lowly minds were madden'd to the height
    By tonguester tricks,
And once – I well remember that red night
    When thirty ricks,

X

All flaming, made as English homestead hell –
    These hands of mine
Have helpt to pass a bucket from the well
    Along the line,

40

XI

When this bare dome had not begun to gleam
    Thro' youthful curls,
And you were then a lover's fairy dream,
    His girl of girls;

XII

And you, that now are lonely, and with Grief
  Sit face to face,
Might find a flickering glimmer of relief
  In change of place.

XIII

What use to brood? This life of mingled pains
  And joys to me,   50
Despite of every Faith and Creed, remains
  The Mystery.

XIV

Let golden youth bewail the friend, the wife,
  For ever gone.
He dreams of that long walk thro' desert life
  Without the one.

XV

The silver year should cease to mourn and sigh —
  Not long to wait —
So close are we, dear Mary, you and I
  To that dim gate.   60

XVI

Take, read! and be the faults your Poet makes
  Or many or few,
He rests content, if his young music wakes
  A wish in you

XVII

To change our dark Queen-city, all her realm
  Of sound and smoke,
For his clear heaven, and these few lanes of elm
  And whispering oak.

TO THE MARQUIS OF DUFFERIN AND AVA

I

At times our Britain cannot rest,
  At times her steps are swift and rash;
  She moving, at her girdle clash
The golden keys of East and West.

II

Not swift or rash, when late she lent
  The sceptres of her West, her East,
  To one, that ruling has increased
Her greatness and her self-content.

III

Your rule has made the people love
  Their ruler. Your viceregal days   10
  Have added fulness to the phrase
Of 'Gauntlet in the velvet glove.'

IV

But since your name will grow with Time,
  Not all, as honouring your fair fame
  Of Statesman, have I made the name
A golden portal to my rhyme:

V

But more, that you and yours may know
  From me and mine, how dear a debt
  We owed you, and are owing yet
To you and yours, and still would owe.   20

VI

For he – your India was his Fate,
  And drew him over sea to you –
  He fain had ranged her through and through,
To serve her myriads and the State, –

188

VII

A soul that, watched from earliest youth,
　　And on through many a brightening year,
　　Had never swerved for craft or fear,
By one side-path, from simple truth;

VIII

Who might have chased and claspt Renown
　　And caught her chaplet here – and there　　　　30
　　In haunts of jungle-poisoned air
The flame of life went wavering down;

IX

But ere he left your fatal shore,
　　And lay on that funereal boat,
　　Dying, 'Unspeakable' he wrote
'Their kindness,' and he wrote no more;

X

And sacred is the latest word;
　　And now the Was, the Might-have-been,
　　And those lone rites I have not seen,
And one drear sound I have not heard,　　　　40

XI

Are dreams that scarce will let me be,
　　Not there to bid my boy farewell,
　　When That within the coffin fell,
Fell – and flashed into the Red Sea,

XII

Beneath a hard Arabian moon
　　And alien stars. To question, why
　　The sons before the fathers die,
Not mine! and I may meet him soon;

XIII

But while my life's late eve endures,
  Nor settles into hueless gray,
  My memories of his briefer day   50
Will mix with love for you and yours.

THE ROSES ON THE TERRACE

Rose, on this terrace fifty years ago,
  When I was in my June, you in your May,
Two words, '*My* Rose' set all your face aglow,
  And now that I am white, and you are gray,
That blush of fifty years ago, my dear,
  Blooms in the Past, but close to me today
As this red rose, which on our terrace here
  Glows in the blue of fifty miles away.

JUNE BRACKEN AND HEATHER

There on the top of the down,
The wild heather round me and over me June's high blue,
When I looked at the bracken so bright and the heather so
      brown,
I thought to myself I would offer this book to you,
This, and my love together,
To you that are seventy-seven,
With a faith as clear as the brights of the June-blue heaven,
And a fancy as summer-new
As the green of the bracken amid the gloom of the heather.

CROSSING THE BAR

Sunset and evening star,
  And one clear call for me!
And may there be no moaning of the bar,
  When I put out to sea,

But such a tide as moving seems asleep,
　　Too full for sound and foam,
When that which drew from out the boundless deep
　　Turns again home.

Twilight and evening bell,
　　And after that the dark!　　　　　　　　10
And may there be no sadness of farewell,
　　When I embark;

For tho' from out our bourne of Time and Place
　　The flood may bear me far,
I hope to see my Pilot face to face
　　When I have crost the bar.

Critical commentary

Although Tennyson's early poems bear marks of the influence of the Romantic poets who were active during his childhood – and especially that of Keats – he quickly established a personal style. Its leading characteristics are the creation of situations that externalize inner feelings, combined with delicacy and precision in the use of language and verse. In the first poem in this selection, for instance, a phrase from Shakespeare is the starting-point for a description that seems to owe something to the Gothic tradition: the woman, abandoned by her lover, is pining away and longing for the release of death in a setting that reflects her own emotional condition. As J. S. Mill pointed out in a highly perceptive review published in 1835, the love story is minimized and the emphasis falls almost entirely on Mariana's isolation and estrangement from human company and human sympathy. There cannot be much doubt that for the young Tennyson this constituted an encoding of his own psychological situation, and it was not to be the last time he would create a situation superficially remote from his own (in time, place, gender, etc.) to express his personal anguish.

At the same time the objectifying of his feelings acts as a restraint upon self-indulgent confession or self-expression, and the setting is created with pictorial vividness:

> The rusted nails fell from the knots
>> That held the pear to the gable-wall.
> The broken sheds look'd sad and strange:
>> Unlifted was the clinking latch;
>> Weeded and worn the ancient thatch
> Upon the lonely moated grange.

One has the sense of a camera moving from one image to another, now in close-up (as in the first line of the passage quoted), now in long shot (as in the last line). Nor is the effect exclusively pictorial, since the remarkable line 'Unlifted was the clinking latch' draws attention to sound (the frequently-lifted latch of a door used by many people), though only to deny it and hence to stress the solitude and inertia of Mariana's plight. Sounds were always to be important for Tennyson, and his concern for verbal musicality is suggested by his revision of the second line quoted, which originally read: 'That held the peach to the garden-wall'; the jettisoning of 'peach', and possibly also of 'garden', seems to have been dictated less by a concern with meaning than by the preference for more muted, less emphatic sounds.

Ultimately, though, all these descriptive details are not there for their own sake but to establish an outer world that is a symbol, metaphor or metonymy for Mariana's state. As we shall see, this is a persistent strategy, especially in Tennyson's early work, and represents an attempt to pass intensely personal writing off as impersonal. It also strikingly anticipates the work of the Pre-Raphaelites a couple of decades later – of, for instance, a poem such as Dante Gabriel Rossetti's 'The Wood-Spurge' – and even of the Symbolist poets at the end of the century.

Several years later, a similar strategy operates more dramatically in the writing of one of Tennyson's best-known short poems, the dramatic monologue 'Ulysses'. This is one of the earliest of his poetic responses to the death of Arthur Hallam, written only two or three weeks after the news reached him. There is nothing surprising about a young poet reaching for his pen on hearing the news of a friend's death, but Tennyson's motive was not to commemorate Hallam but to work out his own internal problems – problems that he could not discuss with anyone close at hand. What he did was far from obvious, for 'Ulysses' is a poem based on the last chapter in the life of the Ancient Greek hero (as told by Dante rather than Homer), a Ulysses whose life of adventure is apparently over but who is determined to embark on one last voyage. The connection with the situation of young Alfred Tennyson is not immediately obvious, but in a sense the central issue of the poem is the hinted-at alternative to living life to the full: if one does *not* make an effort (difficult though it may be) to go on living, the alternative is inertia, withdrawal, melancholy, perhaps suicide. ('The Two Voices', written at about the same time, debates the issue more explicitly.) Characteristically his technique is to use the dramatic monologue – some years before Browning gave greater prominence to the form – to objectify his own intense emotions: between the poet and his reader stands Ulysses and *his* audience, the latter becoming more perceptible as the poem progresses. Thus a young man in nineteenth-century Lincolnshire utilizes a Greek legend, as he was to do again in 'Tithonus' and other poems, to express a personal predicament.

At the same time 'Ulysses' has been seen by modern critics as unwittingly self-revealing, or imperfectly concealing Tennyson's personal feelings, in a contradiction that seems to exist between what the poem is *saying* and what it *enacts*. The 'message' of the poem is a call to action, but the verse itself is exceptionally slow-moving, as if embodying an unconscious undermining of the stated convictions. Matthew Arnold declared (with humorous exaggeration, of course) that lines 19–21 'take up nearly as much time [to read aloud] as a whole book of the *Iliad*', and lines 55–6 are perhaps an even better example of this tendency towards stasis:

The long day wanes: the slow moon climbs: the deep
Moans round with many voices.

Again, Tennyson's control of sound and verse-movement is masterly: the high proportion of monosyllables and stressed syllables, the punctuation breaks within the line, and the preponderance of long vowels all slow down the blank verse almost to stopping-point – and this in a poem that is ostensibly a rallying-cry to a life of energetic action.

'The Lady of Shalott', like 'Mariana', employs the motif of the isolated female, only this time the setting is painstakingly medieval and the poem provides early evidence of Tennyson's lifelong infatuation with the Arthurian cycle of stories. It has, at the same time, an important relationship to his own dilemma at the time at which it was written concerning the direction his poetic career should take. His genius was recognized, at least by his friends, while he was still an undergraduate, and one of his Cambridge contemporaries is reported to have said to him: 'Tennyson, we cannot live in art.' There was perhaps a hint of reproach as well as of well-meant advice in this comment, since Tennyson's early poems (as we have seen) explored and exploited a self-absorbed withdrawal from the world of action. During the ensuing decades, Tennyson was to be the victim of conflicting impulses: an instinctive desire to turn his back on the world (and thus to escape its problems), and the wish dictated by conscience to work for social good. In the course of time the latter gained ground over the former, and the later Tennyson is conspicuously a public poet, responding to many of the central issues of the age. Even so, many of his finest poems in his later years remain intensely personal.

'The Lady of Shalott' is a parable of the artist's isolation – a theme also explored, with a different outcome, in 'The Palace of Art'. Whereas the former suggests that quitting the ivory tower and involving oneself in the world outside exacts a penalty, the latter poem leads to a recognition that the palace of art cannot ultimately satisfy. Yet there is some vacillation or failure of nerve at the end:

> So when four years were wholly finished
>   She threw her royal robes away.
> 'Make me a cottage in the vale,' she said,
>   'Where I may mourn and pray.
>
> 'Yet pull not down my palace towers, that are
>   So lightly, beautifully built:
> Perchance I may return with others there
>   When I have purged my guilt.'

The world of aesthetic self-sufficiency is not entirely renounced: the palace door is left open for a possible return, though with 'others' – a significant commitment to society and the community. In these poems Tennyson is participating in a debate on the relationship between art and life that was to preoccupy many writers and thinkers, from Matthew Arnold to Oscar Wilde, throughout the nineteenth century. (It is indeed still an ongoing issue, involved in, for instance, the argument over pornography.) Yet the ending of 'The Palace of Art' seems to reveal some uncertainty at this stage. Endings were often to present problems for Tennyson, and the two endings of 'The Lady of Shalott' repay careful comparison.

The medievalism of that poem is taken up again in 'Morte

d'Arthur', the longest of all the short-term responses to Hallam's death. Again, the coding mechanism is clearly operating: faced with the loss of an idealized friend called Arthur, Tennyson writes about an idealized legendary king, and the costume-drama remoteness of the setting only serves to conceal the personal motivation. The poem later became (under a new title, 'The Passing of Arthur') the last in the long and ambitious series *Idylls of the King*, Tennyson's long drawn out attempt to create an English epic. The *Idylls* were thus in a sense written backwards. The choice of blank verse had Miltonic precedent, but it has to be said that in these long blank-verse poems the emotional pressure often drops and Tennyson becomes the victim of his own fluency and technical skill. At its weakest the verse can degenerate into prosaic banality or even into periphrastic absurdities recalling Augustan poetic diction (Arthur's moustache is 'the knightly growth that fringed his lips'). Tennyson's problem – and it is one he does not entirely succeed in solving – is to devise a language sufficiently different both from contemporary speech and from the current language of poetry to suggest a remote age and an epic world. Some parts of the poem have genuine drama: for example, the description (lines 176–92) of Sir Bedivere carrying Arthur to the water's edge. Yet even here the effects, brilliant though they are, are too obviously calculated – the insistent onomatopoeia of lines 186–90, and the abrupt contrast of 191–2. What seems to be missing here is the distinctive Tennysonian strengths, including the sharp eye for visual detail (remarkable in one who was severely myopic), the intense interest (at times recalling Gerard Manley Hopkins) in the natural world in all its variety and particularity, and the intensely self-aware analysis of his own states of mind. A case can be made – though certainly not all critics of Tennyson would accept it – that the success of Tennyson's poems is often in inverse proportion to their length and ambitions, and that in many of the longer poems his powerful sensibility and ability to use language with great precision and intensity become dissipated in the quest for large-scale effects.

An important exception to this is the long poems that are in effect composed of shorter poems, especially *In Memoriam* and *Maud*. Also instructive in this connection is *The Princess*, where some of Tennyson's finest lyrics are interpolated in a poem that is concerned with the topical issue of women's education; a somewhat startling effect is produced by the juxtaposition of the long sections of discursive, polemical blank verse – of a kind much more rapid, flexible and conversational than the stately and consciously archaic verse of 'Morte d'Arthur' – and the short intense lyrics such as the desolated 'Tears, idle tears' and the erotic 'Now sleeps the crimson petal'.

With *The Princess*, published in 1847, we can see Tennyson making a major commitment to becoming a public poet and using poetry to confront urgent questions of the day. Yet the interpolated lyrics suggest that he is trying to have it both ways, living in the world outside the palace of art but sneaking back there from time to time for a brief visit. Three years later *In Memoriam* represents a turning-point in his career and qualifies him for the laureateship that is in turn to make demands on him (fulfilled despite initial resistance) to write poems to order for royal events, state occasions and notable happenings (the germ of 'The Charge of the Light Brigade' is a newspaper report). If we think, as we surely should, of different areas of Tennyson's poetry as demanding different voices, that of a poem such as the 'Ode on the Death of the Duke of Wellington' could hardly be more different from that of, say, 'Mariana'; whereas the latter is subdued, intimate and brooding, the former is confidently rhetorical, the voice of one conscious that he is speaking both to and on behalf of a great public.

Part of the strength of *In Memoriam* comes from its being simultaneously a private and a public poem. Its origins go back seventeen years, to the first creative reactions to Hallam's death. It grew slowly and was published with great reluctance and anonymously. The Victorian age, from the Queen downwards, seized on it gratefully as an articulation of shared anxieties over the undermining of faith by new movements, including science. Tennyson's private experience was thus recognized as representative, and in its final form the structure of the poem embodies the various stages of that experience – from loss, grief, shock, resentment, and desolation, through the struggle to reconcile such an apparently meaningless catastrophe with the idea of a loving personal God, to the concluding confident note of acceptance, reconciliation and faith.

Read in its entirety, the poem has an almost novelistic structure (Tennyson was a great reader of novels) with references to the seasons and to anniversaries marking the passage of time. Within this framework the individual lyrics can be read as short poems in their own right, but part of their meaning is derived from the poems that precede and follow them and from their place in the larger design. There is room in this selection for only a handful of the 131 poems, plus Prologue and Epilogue, that constitute *In Memoriam*, but they have been chosen to exemplify the emotional range of the complete work.

Section II, for instance, finds the speaker in a churchyard, contemplating the idea of physical death and dissolution: the yew tree sends down roots and fibres that wrap themselves around the 'dreamless head' and the skeleton of the dead man. It is, with its clear-eyed emphasis on bodily decay and reunion with the chemical cycle, a very nineteenth-century image – unparalleled in, for instance, an otherwise comparable eighteenth-century poem, Gray's *Elegy* – and anticipates the more explicitly scientific stance of Hardy in such poems as 'Transformations' and 'Voices from Things Growing in a Churchyard'. In the last line of the poem, with an unexpected imaginative leap, the speaker, absorbed by his vision and deeply conscious of the contrast between the tree's longevity (line 12) and the brevity of human life (lines 7–8), seems to lose his own identity and become 'incorporate' with the tree – that is, entering into its physical existence and thus (implicitly) attaining a kind of reunion with the dead. Ultimately the image seems to take on a sexual dimension, and Tennyson's feelings for Hallam were certainly intense, though it is probably oversimplifying a complex situation to talk glibly (as some critics have done) about homosexuality. The sexual terminology and even the sexual concepts so familiar to us were unavailable to Tennyson, and an important element in his feelings was romantic idealization of a man whose character and abilities he believed, quite possibly incorrectly, to be superior to his own.

The setting of VII, in contrast, is urban, and the poem is striking for its renunciation of the usual Tennysonian ornateness and musicality – his underwriting of Keats's dictum that 'Poetry should surprise by a fine excess' – in favour of a monochrome bleakness more familiar in the realistic novel. Revisiting Hallam's London home – a ghost himself (the 'guilty thing' of line 7 is an echo of *Hamlet*) seeking a ghost – he is tormented by the sense of 'then and now' created by memory. The final stanza points the irony of a world of action from which the person who means the most to him is missing: a new dawn (traditional symbol of hope and promise for the future) brings only the aching sense of loss and irrecoverable past happiness. The final line, consisting of eight commonplace monosyllabic words, with 'bald' and 'blank' (like 'dark' and 'unlovely' in the first stanza) suggesting negativity and deprivation, slows down the movement of the verse almost to the point of inertia – the inertia of a paralysing depressive state. In both of these poems there seems to be a survival of what was noted in the very early poem 'Mariana' – a blurring of the normal distinction between subjective experience and the objective world whereby internal moods and external scenes take on each other's colouring. W. H. Auden once remarked that there was nothing Tennyson didn't know about melancholia, and certainly he had ample opportunities of observing different kinds and degrees of psychological disturbance both in himself and in members of his own family, beginning in childhood with his father. His pre-Freudian poetry often shows a remarkable insight into abnormal states of mind.

LIV–LVI, in contrast, are passionately argumentative, the verse-movement gathering momentum as it is driven forward by a debate that is not merely intellectual but, as always for Tennyson, intensely personal. Note especially the very long sentence in LVI that begins in line 8 and concludes in line 20 only after rejecting (at least for the moment) traditional Christian beliefs and confronting a Darwinian struggle for existence ('Nature, red in tooth and claw') and a time-scale enlarged by the discoveries of Victorian archaeology (lines 19–20). Again Tennyson anticipates Hardy in being the reluctant inheritor of the hugely expanded vistas of time and space opened up by nineteenth-century science, with the consequent shrinking of human significance; so far from being Nature's 'last work' (line 9) with a unique position among created beings, humanity is relegated to being just one stage in a blind mechanical process, doomed eventually to join the dinosaurs as a superseded species. At such points in the poem Tennyson is voicing with passion and eloquence what innumerable Victorian men and women were struggling with in their own minds and hearts; Queen Victoria was not speaking only for herself when she said that, after the Bible, the poem had been her greatest comfort after her husband's death.

It could provide comfort, however, only by finally endorsing Christian beliefs, including faith in a loving God and in personal survival after death, and in this respect Tennyson differs from Hardy (and from others such as George Eliot) who found the challenges posed by Victorian scepticism unanswerable. By the time we reach XCV, the semi-mystical experience of rereading Hallam's letters – the precise situation delineated like an episode in a novel or an autobiography – constitutes a form of communion with the dead: 'And all at once it seem'd at last/ The living soul was flash'd on mine' (lines 35–6). The dawn at the end of the poem, 'broaden[ing] into boundless day', is symbolic as well as literal and forms a contrast with the hopeless dawn at the end of VII – one of a large number of echoes, cross-references and self-quotations that contribute towards the unity of *In Memoriam*. Similarly, in CXXIII, the 'long street' of line 3 recalls the 'long unlovely street' of VII, and the geologically-informed vision of continents and oceans changing their shape over aeons of time recalls the grim scientific arguments of LIV–LVI. Now, however, faith has regained power not only to 'dream my dream' but to 'hold it true' and to reject the idea that death is the end. The key-word of the last sections of the poem is 'faith', as its earlier portions have been haunted by despair and harrowed by doubt. The poem's concluding lines (below) reject a purely biological view of humanity ('half-akin to brute'), see Hallam as an early manifestation of a higher form of humanity that will emerge in course of time, affirm his personal immortality ('That friend of mine who lives in God'), and insist that progress and a divine plan are the principles of the universe:

No longer half-akin to brute,
   For all we thought and loved and did,
   And hoped, and suffer'd, is but seed
Of what in them is flower and fruit;

Whereof the man, that with me trod
   This planet, was a noble type
   Appearing ere the times were ripe,
That friend of mine who lives in God,

That God, which ever lives and loves,
   One God, one law, one element,
   And one far-off divine event,
To which the whole creation moves.

It goes without saying that such a message was eagerly and gratefully received by Tennyson's contemporaries, and *In Memoriam* established itself as the most popular long poem of the Victorian age. It needs to be added, though, that Tennyson's own religious faith was less impregnable than the above lines might suggest, and that to the end of his life he continued, sometimes desperately, to seek reassurance, especially on the question of survival after death. The popularity of his poem was not simply a matter of its articulation of widely-shared anxieties and its final message of encouragement: there was recognition too of its lyrical and rhetorical power. Its distinctive effects are partly produced by the unusual stanza form, the *abba*-rhyming quatrains which Tennyson did not actually invent but which had been only rarely used in English verse. Whereas most quatrains (*abab* or *abcb*) embody a sense of forward movement, the *In Memoriam* stanza, with its final return to its beginning, produces a hauntingly brooding, even obsessive effect characteristic of Tennyson's mind. At the same time the grand design of the poem creates a sense of forward movement and progression through a series of stages of emotional and intellectual response.

In Memoriam, then, is both a public and a private poem: a document in the Victorian conflict between faith and 'honest doubt' (Tennyson's own phrase), but also a crucial chapter of autobiography, comparable with other classic accounts of intellectual and emotional struggle such as those by J. S. Mill and Edmund Gosse. (Interestingly, it appeared at almost exactly the same time as two other landmarks in autobiographical writing, Wordsworth's *Prelude* and Dickens's *David Copperfield*.) The autobiographical mode, overt or disguised, is to be found in much of Tennyson's best work, and we have seen already how a poem like 'Ulysses' can embody a coded autobiographical statement. The monologue is also a favourite form, though it goes without saying that the 'I' of the monologuist is not necessarily the autobiographical 'I' and may indeed be radically in contrast to it. A dramatic monologue such as 'St Simeon Stylites' creates a deliberately unsympathetic, even repugnant character whose condemnation by the reader is based on his own words: as with Browning's 'My Last Duchess' or 'The Bishop Orders his Tomb', what is in question is not merely indictment but self-indictment. The self-appointed martyr, whose pretence of Christian humility and submissiveness is an unsuccessful disguise for his self-conceit and self-glorification, condemns himself through his rhetoric: the language of the opening lines, with the superlative of 'the basest of mankind' and the lurid imagery of the second line, immediately set the tone for a character who resembles some of Dickens's religious hypocrites. Very different in language and tone is 'Tithonus', based on a story of classical rather than Christian origin and embodying Tennyson's long-standing anxiety about immortality. To compare these two dramatic monologues is to gain a sense of the range of 'voices' that Tennyson could create and to be reminded of his interest in the drama, and in particular his idolization of Shakespeare. The late poem 'Rizpah' is an interesting experiment in using the language of a working-class woman to bring a Biblical story up to date and to demonstrate that basic human situations recur throughout the ages regardless of time and place. Elsewhere (not included in this selection) Tennyson also wrote poems utilizing the Lincolnshire dialect with which he had been familiar since boyhood. (Throughout life he seems to have spoken with a broad Lincolnshire accent.)

A monologue with more obviously personal elements is 'Locksley Hall', and Tennyson's insistence that it was *not* autobiographical may serve to confirm our suspicions that it is. At this stage of his life (in his late twenties) he certainly had plenty to complain about, or at least to be unhappy about, and the poem is too close to the personal emotions that generated it to be an artistic success. One Victorian reader (R. W. Dixon, the friend of G. M. Hopkins) commented that it merely produced the effect of 'a man making an unpleasant and rather ungentlemanly row', and a modern critic, Christopher Ricks, has judged it 'histrionic'. For all his reclusiveness, Tennyson had something of the actor in his nature – his recitations of his own poems were notably dramatic – and Victorian acting styles were of course overstated and even hammy by modern standards. In these dramatic monologues he often seems to be experimenting with the effect of different voices, and if the experiments are sometimes unsuccessful that is not surprising. Metrically speaking, the poem uses a very uncommon form: long lines of fifteen syllables rhyming in pairs. The escape from blank verse is to be welcomed, and in the short run the lines achieve something of the tempo of the spoken language; but in a poem of this length the form lacks variety and the ultimate effect of the unrelenting trochaic measure is of a monotonous jingle. A later poem, 'In the Children's Hospital', uses a similar verse-form as the medium for much less personal material, a social documentary that can be paralleled in Victorian fiction.

In *Maud*, an unusually long dramatic monologue, variety is achieved by the division into sections and subsections that make use of a wide variety of verse-forms. In Tennyson's terms the poem is a 'monodrama' – he also described it as 'a little *Hamlet*', since the hero's temporary madness or mental breakdown is involved – but the monotony of the single voice is avoided and a considerable range of moods is expressed. The opening conveys passionate feelings in a manner that recalls 'Locksley Hall', though the language and imagery are now richer and more fully under control:

> I hate the dreadful hollow behind the little wood,
> Its lips in the field above are dabbled with blood-red heath,
> The red-ribb'd ledges drip with a silent horror of blood,
> And Echo there, whatever is ask'd her, answers 'Death'.

A few lines later, a phrase like 'the flying gold of the ruin'd woodlands' has a remarkable intensity, the 'gold' being both the autumn leaves and the lost fortune, with 'flying' and 'ruin'd' reinforcing the ambiguity.

The speaker's personal bitterness and indignation soon give way to a more objective exposure of the abuses inflicted by the rich and powerful on the poor: such topics as the adulteration of food and the sale of harmful drugs as medicines gain entry to the poem in a way that would never have happened in the earliest stages of Tennyson's career. By 1854 poetry has become for Tennyson not just a means of self-expression and self-therapy but a means of discharging a social responsibility, and his growing fame and readership are making him increasingly conscious of the powers wielded by a writer. Auden's dictum that poetry makes nothing happen would have found no assent from Tennyson. There is also room for a return to the impact of the new science that had been touched on in *In Memoriam*, only the treatment is now more rhetorical:

> A monstrous eft was of old the Lord and Master of Earth,
> For him did his high sun flame, and his river billowing ran,

And he felt himself in his force to be Nature's crowning race.
As nine months go to the shaping an infant ripe for his birth,
So many a million of ages have gone to the making of man:
He now is first, but is he the last? is he not too base?

The lines are almost twice as long as those of the earlier poem, the stanzas half as long again with a rhyme-scheme (*abcabc*) that thrusts forward: the voice is now not privately musing but publicly declaiming, and there is an irony (in the first three lines quoted) that in its mocking tone has no parallel in *In Memoriam*. For examples of very different moods later in the poem compare, for instance, the love lyric 'Come into the garden, Maud' (especially the tenth stanza), the narrative section at the beginning of Part II, with its relatively short lines and direct, even colloquial language, and the extreme simplicity of 'See what a lovely shell' shortly afterwards, with its poignant sense of a mind that has recovered its balance after a period of disturbance. (Tennyson's own note on this last section reads: 'The shell undestroyed amid the storm perhaps symbolises to him his own first and highest nature preserved amid the storms of passion.')

The linguistic and metrical variety of *Maud* make it in some respects a very modern poem, and there are lines that could have found a place in the early poems of T. S. Eliot (who, incidentally, wrote an important essay on *In Memoriam*):

Then I rise, the eavedrops fall,
And the yellow vapours choke
The great city sounding wide;
The day comes, a dull red ball
Wrapt in drifts of lurid smoke
On the misty river-tide.

In this externalization of subjective mood through the depiction of the vast anonymous city, where fog and smoke pollute even the sunrise, *Maud* is much closer to *The Love Song of J. Alfred Prufrock* and *The Waste Land* than to Wordsworth's sonnet 'Upon Westminster Bridge'.

For Tennyson himself, *Maud* had a very special place in his large œuvre, and it was the poem he most liked to read or recite, doing so on many recorded occasions over many years. Its dramatic quality makes it a more obviously suitable case for such treatment than, say, *In Memoriam*, but this in itself hardly seems sufficient to account for the almost obsessive eagerness with which Tennyson would declaim it over and over again; it seems likely that in addition there was something in the hero's experience of mental disturbance and recovery of equilibrium that corresponded to his own experience, actual or perceived as potential. It may have been a recognition, too, of the nature of the psychological experience explored in the poem that made many contemporary critics uneasy about *Maud* – though uneasy is hardly a strong enough word, for some of the reviews and responses were vitriolic. (One comment was that the title contained one vowel too many, and it didn't matter which one was omitted.) There were frequent complaints about the poem's obscurity – another clue to its modernity.

Against the hostility aroused by *Maud* can be set the enormous critical and popular success of *Enoch Arden* in the next decade, and while the former has gained in reputation in more recent times the latter remains decidedly out of fashion. It is instructive to enquire, therefore, what elements in the respective critical climates of the mid-Victorian age and our own may have produced such divergent judgments. From its very opening lines, with their nervously emphatic rhythms, *Maud* is directly expressive of abnormal states of mind, the violent swings from one mood to another being reflected in the changing verse-forms. *Enoch Arden* on the other hand is related by an objective narrator and cast in blank verse that is curiously and consciously old-fashioned and prosaic in the style of, say, Wordsworth's *Michael*. (It is significant that one of the likely models is a poem 'The Parting Hour', one of the *Tales in Verse* published in 1812 by the severely realistic poet George Crabbe. Crabbe exposed the conditions of life for the poor on the East Anglian coast, the setting of Tennyson's poem.)

Tennyson seems to have set himself to renounce the verbal richness and musicality that had been hallmarks of much of his earlier work, and to write something comparable to what had been done in the contemporary novel of realism. (In *David Copperfield* Dickens had described the lives of East Anglian fisherfolk, and Elizabeth Gaskell used plot-situations very similar to the central issue of *Enoch Arden* in a short story of 1858, 'The Manchester Marriage'.) The

tale of humble life, then, is matched by language that is calculat-
edly, even jarringly naive. But there is more to *Enoch Arden* than a
perfunctory reading might suggest. Although set in an earlier period,
it is in fact highly topical in its concern with the plight of the indi-
vidual who, mistakenly but sincerely believing a spouse to be dead,
contracts a bigamous marriage. This was not at all a rare occurrence
at a time when travel to a remote part of the world might separate
spouses for long periods, and the Offences Against the Person Act
of 1861, which came into law at just about the time Tennyson was
conceiving his poem, contained legislation bearing on this point. In
its topicality no less than in its exposure of the hardships suffered
by the poor – for all Enoch's troubles stem from economic prob-
lems – *Enoch Arden* affirms Tennyson's commitment to being a public
poet prepared to use his gifts and status, as Dickens and Gaskell had
used theirs in fiction, for propagandist purposes.

A careful examination of the structure of the poem suggests, too,
that it is not quite as artless and 'natural' as it may at first appear,
and that contemporary readers who reacted primarily to its senti-
ment and its social indignation were attending to the message at the
expense of the medium. It is in fact, through its repetitive and
symbolic narrative patterns, an intricately constructed work: what
looks at first like a realistic short story in verse turns out to be an
elaborately patterned narrative in which almost every significant event
is paralleled elsewhere in the poem, and dramatic irony is certainly
not absent. The latter half of the poem can be read, indeed, as an
ironic replay of the first half: as the children (two boys and a girl)
play together in the opening lines, Annie innocently promises that
'she would be little wife to both' and spends the rest of the poem
unwittingly living up to that promise; as a young sailor Enoch three
times rescues a drowning man, to be later himself one of three
survivors of a shipwreck; he works hard to buy a boat, but has to
sell it when financial problems beset him; Philip is the unseen viewer
of Enoch and Annie's happiness, but the roles are reversed near the
end when Enoch returns and sees his place in the home occupied
by the other man; Philip's proposal takes place in the same wood,
and at the same time of year, as Enoch's; Enoch, believed to be
dead, returns to life only to find he is unwanted and to condemn
himself to a real death; dying, he relives in his delirium the rescue
from the island that has turned out to be no piece of good luck

but a tragic misfortune, and dies with the ironic ambiguous cry 'I am saved'. The list could be extended and a careful reading will reveal other instances of patterning.

There are also verbal repetitions – for instance, the two scenes that take place in a wood both contain the characteristic but (in this poem) exceptionally romantic lines 'Just where the prone edge of the wood began/ To feather toward the hollow . . .', and the two weddings (only the second is of course no real wedding) are both accompanied by the line 'So these were wed, and merrily rang the bells' ('merrily' acquiring an ironic force on the line's second appearance).

With all this in mind we may wish to think again about the poem's ending – a conclusion that has been condemned and ridiculed for its banality and tactlessness by generations of readers:

> So past the strong heroic soul away.
> And when they buried him the little port
> Had seldom seen a costlier funeral.

The final emphasis on the cost of the funeral has often been judged a piece of crass and wildly inappropriate materialism, but should surely be seen as ironic. Money, as already noted, has been the source of all Enoch's troubles, and now that it is freely available (for Annie has 'married' a prosperous man) it is too late to do him any good. It is known that Tennyson strongly disapproved of the elaborateness of conventional mid-Victorian mourning customs, and there is general criticism as well as local irony in the line. To call Enoch 'heroic', however, is a deliberately provocative challenge: there is nothing self-evident about the heroism of this obscure man who dies unknown, and indeed his heroism consists finally in doing nothing, in remaining silent; but Tennyson is insisting that heroism can be found not only in Ulysses and King Arthur but in an obscure provincial community.

On first publication *Enoch Arden* was a remarkable popular and commercial success: 17,000 copies of the volume of which it is the title-poem were sold on the day of publication (probably more than most present-day poets sell in a lifetime). Many reviewers were rhapsodical in their eulogies, and it quickly became absorbed into popular culture through adaptations: as an item for reading aloud, as a subject for illustration (including a fine drawing by Edward Lear), in versions for the stage and later the silent cinema (there were at least three stage and four screen versions). It was, too, enormously popular in America and was translated into at least 28 foreign languages. One biographer has gone so far as to describe it as the most popular poem Tennyson ever wrote. All this is in stark contrast to its treatment, denigratory or indifferent, in later generations. Twentieth-century schools of criticism have encouraged approaches and techniques that favour the short poem and disadvantage the long poem, which has in any case gone out of fashion among modern poets. To turn to *Enoch Arden* today is to be challenged to respond to a work of an unfamiliar kind, and one that is considerably more complex both in its formal qualities and in the issues it raises than may at first appear.

Near the end of this selection is a group of poems not all of which are in their strict chronological position. They have been placed together because they are all short, personal poems addressed to named or easily identifiable individuals and are tributes to relationships and friendships that have often extended over many years. Characteristically they enable Tennyson, from a vantage-point in old age, to look back over his lifetime and to explore and relive his memories of the past. Even when turbulent emotions are being recalled, the tone of these poems is cool, relaxed, poised – a Wordsworthian emotion recollected in tranquillity, but, unlike the Wordsworthian model, a steady contemplation of the past rather than a reliving of it. If we compare these poems with such early poems as 'Mariana' or 'The Two Voices', we gain a sense of how far Tennyson has travelled in his long career in control of his feelings and of the language in which they are expressed; there is something classical (and specifically Horatian) or Augustan about these letters in verse addressed to old (in some instances dead) friends. No longer does he find it necessary to resort to the persona of a dramatic monologue, but can speak out in his own voice – a voice that moves flexibly between regret, nostalgia, affection, wit, humour, and self-knowledge.

Two of the finest of these are 'To E. FitzGerald' and 'The Roses on the Terrace'. The former shows remarkable syntactic control, consisting as it does of a single sentence 56 lines long and accommodating a range of associations that includes the memory of his last visit to FitzGerald's home, complimentary references to his translation of the Persian poet Omar Khayyám, a partly self-mocking joke about Fitz's vegetarianism, and above all a commemoration of the friendship that had survived the years since they were undergraduates together. The conclusion, recalling FitzGerald's role in encouraging him to publish his poems, is magnanimous without being fulsome: a delicate point to negotiate, since Tennyson's success and fame had been on so much larger a scale than his friend's. In such a poem the self-absorption, neurotic and even morbid, of some of the earlier work has been entirely left behind.

'The Roses on the Terrace' is a shorter and subtler poem that exploits the lucky accident of Rosa Baring's Christian name. Rosa had been loved and lost by the young Tennyson, and his distress and bitterness found outlets in *Maud* and 'Locksley Hall', where his frustration was presented not just as a personal tragedy but as evidence of the materialism and prejudice of the socially advantaged. (Rosa was the daughter of a wealthy family that owned a country house not far from the Tennysons' modest home.) A lifetime later, however, no trace of bitterness remains: the ravaging emotions of the past are distanced by time, place and memory. In a series of linked visual images the Rose of the present becomes the Rose of 'fifty years ago', his remembered words (' "*My* Rose" ') revive the memory of a rose-like blush, and the 'red rose' blooming before him dissolves cinematically into a symbol of the past as it is seen against the background of a landscape that stretches for miles ('fifty miles' echoing 'fifty years'). It is a poem that in its eight lines makes rich and dense use of colour, ('white', 'gray' and 'blue' as well as the all-pervading red), of repetition ('rose' three times, 'terrace' and 'fifty years ago' twice each), and above all of wordplay whereby the beauty of the 'red rose' becomes identified with the beauty, unfading in memory, of Rose herself. Tennyson's control over his medium is as complete by now as his control over his emotions; again the poem consists of a single sentence, and the slightly unexpected rhyme-scheme (not alternating rhymes, since the second line of each pair ends with a rhyme that unfailingly returns us to line 2) creates a subtle effect of stasis. It is not, however, the reluctant, world-weary condition expressed by the verse of 'Ulysses' but a poise derived from experience and self-knowledge.

A concluding comment may single out two of the shortest poems in this selection. 'Flower in the Crannied Wall' (the first line of the untitled poem) has the air of a spontaneous fragment, its rhythms close to those of natural speech. Paradoxically, though, the subject of this tiny poem is vast and universal: 'what God and man is'. There is an impressive humility in the famous poet's recognition, after a lifetime of intellectual questing, that the answer may be held by an insignificant weed. Again, what appears to be a simple poem is in fact technically accomplished: the unusual rhyme-scheme (*abccab*) seems to return us, perplexed, to the point at which we started, and the internal rhymes ('root and all' with 'wall') and repetition of 'root and all' create a sense of the question echoing endlessly in the mind.

'Flower in the Crannied Wall', which expresses a kind of agnosticism, is less well known – for understandable reasons – than a poem affirming his faith. 'Crossing the Bar' repeats more concisely the comforting message of the conclusion of *In Memoriam*. In contrast to the simple, Wordsworthian image of the flower (Wordsworth's 'the meanest flower that blows can give/ Thoughts that do often lie too deep for tears' was perhaps an unconscious source), we have the dramatic and portentous symbol of 'crossing the bar', invoking the traditional association of the ocean with eternity. Based on a commonplace experience that Tennyson, as a resident of the Isle of Wight, must have undergone innumerable times, 'Crossing the Bar' transcends its origins and in a dozen lines acquires mythic status for the situation it creates. It was appropriate that the magazine *Punch* should have adapted it for a cartoon on the occasion of Tennyson's death: another example (and there are many such) of the absorption of certain elements in Tennyson's work by popular culture. He was perhaps the last practitioner of high poetic art to be accorded this treatment, a fact that says something about the centrality of poetry in Victorian middle-class culture and its marginality in our own.

We have seen that the contemporary success of poems like *In Memoriam* and *Enoch Arden* was on a scale hard to parallel in any age: there had been nothing like it in England since Byron's early successes, and there has certainly been nothing like it since. In his later years – and he lived to a great age – and as his output dwindled, there was some waning of his reputation, but his death was a national event, his funeral in Westminster Abbey a state occasion,

211

and a characteristic verdict on his life and career at the time was that he was the most famous man in England. He suffered – like other Victorian writers, including Dickens and George Eliot, who had enjoyed great contemporary fame – from an inevitable and lengthy period of neglect in the early part of the twentieth century: modernism favoured a very different kind of poetry from Tennyson's. In the past thirty years, however, a large-scale revaluation of Tennyson as thinker and artist has taken place. He has come to be seen as speaking for a complex and tormented age (for facile generalizations about the self-confidence of the Victorians will no longer hold water), and he did so in language that is often subtle, ironic and delicately controlled and with an extraordinary technical mastery of diction, syntax and verse-forms. Like Wordsworth, Browning and many others he produced a vast amount of work, belonging as he did to an age that considered bulk to be one of the hallmarks of a major writer and that would have found the modest dimensions of the work of some modern poets a matter for disparagement. Not all of his poems retain their vitality, and he can be strident or pedestrian. To some extent he is a writer who positively gains from selection. At his best – in, for instance, his depiction of scenes expressing certain moods, in his minutely detailed evocation of the English countryside, in some of his love lyrics, and in his passionately argued debating of issues of faith and doubt – his individual voice is unmistakable, his rendering of emotional states very powerful, and his control of his medium absolute. If he represented in some respects the end of a tradition – an old order (to adapt his own words) that inevitably gave place to new in the work of Hardy, Hopkins, Yeats, Eliot, and others – it was a great tradition and a worthy end.

Reading list

TEXT

Ricks, Christopher (ed.), *The Poems of Tennyson*, 3 vols, London, 1987.

Shatto, Susan (ed.), *Tennyson's 'Maud': A Definitive Edition*, London, 1986.

Shatto, Susan and Shaw, Marion (eds), *Tennyson: 'In Memoriam'*, Oxford, 1982.

Lord Tennyson, Hallam (ed.), *The Works of Tennyson Annotated*, 9 vols, London, 1907–8 (the 'Eversley' edition).

BIOGRAPHY

Martin, Robert Bernard, *Tennyson: The Unquiet Heart*, Oxford and London, 1980.

Nicolson, Harold, *Tennyson: Aspects of his Life, Character and Poetry*, London, 1923.

Ormond, Leonée, *Alferd Tennyson: A Literary Life*, London, 1993.

Page, Norman, *Tennyson: An Illustrated Life*, London, 1992.

Page, Norman (ed.), *Tennyson: Interviews and Recollections*, London, 1983.

Tennyson, Charles, *Alfred Tennyson*, London, 1949.

Lord Tennyson, Hallam, *Alfred Lord Tennyson: A Memoir by his Son*, 2 vols, London, 1897.

Wheatcroft, Andrew, *The Tennyson Album*, London, 1980.

Buckley, Jerome Hamilton, *Tennyson: The Growth of a Poet*, Cambridge, Mass., 1960.

Colley, Ann C., *Tennyson and Madness*, Athens, Georgia, 1983.

Jordan, Elaine, *Alfred Tennyson*, Cambridge, 1988.

Jump, John D. (ed.), *Tennyson: The Critical Heritage*, London, 1967.

Killham, John (ed.), *Critical Essays on the Poetry of Tennyson*, London, 1960.

Palmer, D. J. (ed.), *Tennyson*, London, 1973.

Pitt, Valerie, *Tennyson Laureate*, London, 1962.

Priestley, F. E. L., *Language and Structure in Tennyson's Poetry*, London, 1973.

Rader, R. W., *Tennyson's 'Maud': The Biographical Genesis*, Berkeley, California, 1963.

Ricks, Christopher, *Tennyson*, London, 1972.

Shannon, Edgar Finley, *Tennyson and the Reviewers*, Cambridge, Mass., 1952.

Shaw, Marion, *Alfred Lord Tennyson*, London, 1988.

Shaw, W. David, *Tennyson's Style*, Ithaca & London, 1976.

Sinfield, Alan, *Alfred Tennyson*, Oxford, 1986.

Turner, Paul, *Tennyson*, London, 1976.

Notes

MARIANA

Published in 1830, with minor revisions in later editions. The epigraph is a near-quotation from Shakespeare's *Measure for Measure*, III, 1: 'There, at the moated grange, resides this dejected Mariana', where the reference is to a woman abandoned by the lover who has promised to marry her. The combination of solitude, isolation, melancholy and the death-wish acted as a powerful stimulus on Tennyson's imagination. An early reviewer, W. J. Fox (*Westminster Review*, January 1831), noted that the entire poem 'is generated by the legitimate process of poetical creation, as that process is conducted in a philosophical mind, from a half sentence in Shakespeare'. Charles Kingsley (*Fraser's Magazine*, September 1850) commented on the reliance on 'short and Saxon words'. In a very interesting discussion of the poem (*London Review*, July 1835) J. S. Mill praised Tennyson's 'power of *creating* scenery, in keeping with some state of human feeling; so fitted to it as to be the embodied symbol of it, and to summon up the state of feeling itself, with a force not to be surpassed by anything but reality'. 'Mariana' has been described as a Pre-Raphaelite poem written nearly twenty years before the founding of the Pre-Raphaelite Brotherhood.

4   Tennyson originally wrote 'That held the peach to the garden-wall', changing 'peach' to 'pear' when he reprinted the poem in 1862 and 'garden' to 'gable' in 1869.

Published in 1830.

THE LADY OF SHALOTT

Published in 1832 and extensively revised (see examples below) for republication in 1842. The poem is a very early instance of Tennyson's lifelong interest in the Arthurian stories – an interest manifested soon afterwards in his 'Morte d'Arthur' and much later in his ambitious *Idylls of the King*.

6–9   Compare the original (1832) version of these lines:
        The yellowleavèd waterlily,
        The greensheathèd daffodilly,
        Tremble in the water chilly,
          Round about Shalott.

46–51   Compare the 1832 version:
        She lives with little joy or fear.
        Over the water, running near,
        The sheepbell tinkles in her ear.
        Before her hangs a mirror clear,
          Reflecting towered Camelot.
        And, as the mazy web she whirls,

46   Ricks notes that 'The mirror is not there simply for the fairy-tale; it was set behind the tapestry so that the worker could see the effect from the right side', and points out the influence of Spenser's *Faerie Queene*, III, 2, with its description of a 'Towre' and a 'wondrous myrrhour'.

163–71   Compare the 1832 ending:
        They crossed themselves, their stars they blest,
        Knight, minstrel, abbot, squire and guest.
        There lay a parchment on her breast,
        That puzzled more than all the rest,
          The wellfed wits at Camelot.
        'The web was woven curiously
        The charm is broken utterly,
        Draw near and fear not – this is I,
          The Lady of Shalott.'

The changed ending was probably in response to J. S. Mill's comment on the poem's 'lame and impotent conclusion' in an otherwise favourable review of it (July 1835).

THE PALACE OF ART

Published in 1832 and revised for republication in 1842. Tennyson's friend James Spedding commented (*Edinburgh Review*, April 1843) that the poem 'represents allegorically the condition of a mind which, in the love of beauty and the triumphant consciousness of knowledge and intellectual supremacy, in the intense enjoyment of its own power and glory has lost sight of its relation to man and to God'.

113	*engrailed* a heraldic term meaning 'serrated'
171	*Memnon* a celebrated statue at Thebes in ancient Greece; struck by the rays of the rising sun, it is said to have produced a sound.
227	*'Mene, mene'* an allusion to the Old Testament (*Daniel*, 5), where these are the opening words of the inscription that appears on the wall at Belshazzar's feast and foretells that king's downfall.

THE LOTOS-EATERS

Written in 1830 and published in 1832, with revisions for its reappearance in the 1842 volumes. Tennyson's source for this retelling of a classical legend was Homer's *Odyssey*, where Odysseus and his crew visit the land of the lotos-eaters; those who eat the fruit of the lotos lose all desire to continue the voyage and to return to their homes, but are content to remain in a permanent state of inaction.

8	Tennyson said that this line was based on a waterfall in the Pyrenees, visited with Hallam 'when I was 20 or 21' (see also the next note).
42	Tennyson said that he composed this line on the voyage from Bordeaux to Dublin after his visit to Spain with Hallam in the summer of 1830.
133	*amaranth* an imaginary flower that never dies.

moly a herb with magic properties given by Hermes to Odysseus to counteract the spells of the enchantress Circe.

THE GARDENER'S DAUGHTER

Written in 1833–4, published in 1842. In this loosely autobiographical poem, the narrator may be approximately identified with Tennyson himself, Eustace with Arthur Hallam, and Juliet with Tennyson's sister Emily, to whom Hallam became engaged. The heroine's name is an obvious Shakespearean echo, and the blank verse owes much to the style of Shakespeare's early plays. As often, the young Tennyson uses a narrator who, rather than speaking directly of his emotions, recollects them in old age.

116   *garden-glasses* glass placed over plants to encourage growth.
         glanced Tennyson introduced this revision (all earlier editions have 'shone') in 1890, very near the end of his life.

THE TWO VOICES

Although it has usually been assumed that this poem was written under the impact of Hallam's death – that is, not earlier than the autumn of 1833 – Ricks has shown that it was begun the previous June, though it appears to have been completed later in the year. An earlier title was 'Thoughts of a Suicide'. Published in the 1842 collection.

1   *still small voice* the Biblical phrase is used ironically here, since in the Old Testament it refers to the voice of God.
457   *And all so variously wrought* another example of Tennyson in his old age meticulously improving an early poem: the line was first printed thus in 1884, earlier editions reading 'So variously seemed all things wrought'.

ST SIMEON STYLITES

Written in 1833, published in 1842. This dramatic monologue – 'Browningesque before Browning' in Jerome Hamilton Buckley's phrase – depicts 'a self-satisfied martyr who has enjoyed his suffering in the faith, never as fixed as he has proclaimed it, that he has won salvation' (Buckley, *Tennyson: The Growth of a Poet*, p.26). Buckley suggests that Tennyson may have been making a punning allusion to Charles Simeon, a well-known Evangelical preacher at Cambridge when Tennyson was an undergraduate. The original Simeon Stylites was a Syrian monk of the fifth century and the first of the ascetics who spent their days at the top of a pillar. Tennyson, who was fond of reading the poem aloud, may have used as sources William Hone's *Every-Day Book* (1825) and Edward Gibbon's *Decline and Fall of the Roman Empire*. James Spedding, reviewing the 1842 *Poems* in the *Edinburgh Review* (April 1843), wrote that 'As the "Palace of Art" represents the pride of voluptuous enjoyment in its noblest form, the "St Simeon Stylites" represents the pride of asceticism in its basest.'

81   *lameness, palsies* one of many Biblical allusions in the poem, the reference here being to *Acts* VIII,7. Other echoes are in lines 83, 107, 118, 122, etc. As a clergyman's son, Tennyson knew the Bible well from childhood.

169   *Abaddon and Asmodeus* further Biblical references: Abaddon is 'the angel of the bottomless pit', Asmodeus an evil spirit. Cf. Milton *Paradise Lost*, Bk 4, ll.167–9: 'Than Asmodeus with the fishy fume,/That drove him, though enamoured, from the spouse/Of Tobit's son'. Asmodeus was leader of the fourth order of devils (there were nine orders) and was a malicious devil associated with revenge.

ULYSSES

Written 20 October 1833, less than three weeks after Tennyson learned the news of Hallam's death. Published in 1842. Another dramatic monologue in which the speaker is an old man in a remote period and place. Tennyson was recorded as saying much later that the poem 'gives the feeling about the need of going forward and braving the struggle of life', but it has been pointed out that while the poem affirms that need, its style and movement enact a lethargy or refusal to 'go forward'. Tennyson would have known the story of Ulysses from Homer's *Odyssey*, but a more important influence here is Dante's *Inferno* (Canto 26), which he had probably read in H. F. Cary's translation.

19–21   Ricks quotes Matthew Arnold's hyperbolic observation on these lines that 'It is no blame to their rhythm, which belongs to another order of movement than Homer's, but it is true that these three lines by themselves take up nearly as much time as a whole book of the *Iliad*.' Some might consider that the movement in lines 53–5 comes even closer to reaching a standstill.

63   *Happy Isles* The Isles of the Blest were believed to lie beyond the Pillars of Hercules (now Gibraltar) at the western end of the Mediterranean, hence beyond the limits of the known world.

TIRESIAS

Although not published until 1885, this poem was, according to Hallam Tennyson, 'partly written' at the same time as *Ulysses* – that is, in late 1833, and as part of the immediate creative response to the death of Arthur Hallam. Tennyson's wife writes in a letter of 14 August 1883: 'Ally has been finishing one of his old world poems begun about the *Ulysses* period and discarded.' A few weeks earlier he had heard of the death of his old friend Edward FitzGerald soon after writing a poem to him (given in this selection); the word 'this' in line 50 of the poem to FitzGerald refers to *Tiresias*. In the 1885 volume *Tiresias and Other Poems*, the poem to FitzGerald stands first and is immediately followed by *Tiresias*.

In Greek mythology, Tiresias was a blind prophet fated to tell the truth but not to be believed. One of the stories told to account for his blindness was that he had been struck blind by the goddess Athene after seeing her bathing.

BREAK, BREAK, BREAK

Probably written in the spring of 1834, and one of the many poetic responses to Hallam's death. Published in 1842.

'Morte d'Arthur', written in 1833–4, was yet another of the responses to the death of another Arthur, Tennyson's friend Hallam, and was published in 1842. It was Tennyson's first major work to deal with the legendary king and in an expanded form, and retitled 'The Passing of Arthur', later became the final poem in *Idylls of the King*. Tennyson's main source was Malory's *Morte d'Arthur* XXI, though there are also numerous echoes of Homer (see 'The Epic', line 39) and Virgil that seem to point to Tennyson's aspirations to write an English epic. 'The Epic', which has a contemporary setting (see, for instance, the references to geology and ecclesiastical controversy in line 16) and is written in a conversational style that contrasts with the archaism of the poem within the frame, was written later, probably in 1837–8. According to Tennyson's friend Edward FitzGerald he hoped to forestall criticism thereby ('to anticipate or excuse the "faint Homeric echoes" ' and 'to give a reason for telling an old-world tale').

'The Epic'

40   *chaff and draff* literally, husks left over after the grain has been removed.

'Morte d'Arthur'

1   *So* the opening word implies that the narrative is being resumed rather than begun.

4   *Lyonnesse* Tennyson revived this ancient name (used in Spenser's *Faerie Queene*) for the mythical land between Land's End in Cornwall and the Scilly Isles, and traditionally the home of King Arthur. Tennyson (and later Hardy) uses it to refer to Cornwall itself.

83   Tennyson added this line for the 1853 edition of the poem.

WALKING TO THE MAIL

This dialogue poem was published in 1842 but probably written in 1837–8. An experiment in a deliberately undramatic conversational style (and interesting to compare in this respect with the use of archaic speech in the roughly contemporary 'Morte d'Arthur'), it refers to recent political events including the 1832 Reform Bill (line 59) and the Chartist agitations of 1838 (line 63).

LOCKSLEY HALL

Ricks, following R. W. Rader, suggests the likely date of composition as 1837–8. Published in 1842. Despite Tennyson's insistence that the poem depicts 'an imaginary place and imaginary hero', it has been widely read as partly autobiographical. The prototype of the Hall may be Harrington Hall, not far from the Tennyson family home at Somersby and for a time the home of Rosa Baring, whose wealthy family were disinclined to encourage Tennyson when he fell in love with her in 1834. She married in 1838 and was later recalled in *Maud* and in the very late poem 'The Roses on the Terrace'.

3	Tennyson's revision of 1843 makes the first half of this line less architecturally precise, just as the 1842 reading was itself less precise than the manuscript version. The manuscript reads 'Round the gable, round the turret', revised in 1842 to ''Tis the place, and round the gables'.
75–6	*the poet* Dante, whose *Inferno* is alluded to.
155	*Mahratta* an Indian people.
180	*Joshua* see *Joshua* X,12 (" "Sun, stand thou still upon Gibeon; and thou, Moon, in the valley of Ajalon." And the sun stood still, and the moon stayed.').
182	A celebrated error as well as an up-to-the-minute image: the metaphor is from the newly-introduced railway. Tennyson and Hallam had travelled from Liverpool to Manchester in 1830 on their way back from Spain, that line having just been opened, and (as he later admitted) Tennyson 'thought that the wheels ran in a groove'.
184	*Cathay* China.

THE PRINCESS

Tennyson's long poem on the education of women, published on Christmas Day 1847 and later revised and expanded, is represented here only by three of the interspersed lyrics. 'The splendour falls on castle walls' was, according to Tennyson, 'Written after hearing the echoes at Killarney [in Ireland] in 1848' (the poem was added to *The Princess* in 1850). On a later visit to the same spot Tennyson was told that the popularity of the poem had contributed to the prosperity of the area as a tourist attraction. Benjamin Britten's 'Serenade' includes a setting of this poem. 'Tears, idle tears' was inspired by an autumn visit to Tintern Abbey; it has been pointed out that Hallam's grave at Clevedon, Somerset, is not far away. The poem was attacked by F. R. Leavis in an influential essay ('"Thought" and Emotional Quality: Notes in the Analysis of Poetry', *Scrutiny* XIII, 1945–6) that contrasts it with D. H. Lawrence's 'Piano', and defended by Cleanth Brooks in what became a classic essay of the American New Criticism, 'The Motivation of Tennyson's Weeper' (included in Brooks's *The Well-Wrought Urn* [1947] and reprinted in many collections of critical essays). 'Now sleeps the crimson petal' is based on a Persian poetic form known as the *ghazal*. In line 7, Danae is, in Greek mythology, the maiden to whom the god Zeus appeared in a shower of gold.

IN MEMORIAM A.H.H.

The 'A.H.H.' of the title is, of course, Tennyson's friend Arthur Henry Hallam. The poem was published anonymously in May 1850 but Tennyson's authorship became common knowledge almost at once; nevertheless, none of the numerous editions published during his lifetime carried his name. Tennyson had worked at it, on and off, over the preceding sixteen and a half years. The title was suggested by Emily Tennyson, whom Tennyson married in the month following publication. Tennyson regarded himself as the inventor of the stanza-form, with its distinctive repeated flow and ebb effected by the *abba* rhyme-scheme, and he was disconcerted when, thirty years after publication, a critic pointed out that the form had been anticipated by Renaissance poets. Ricks notes that Shakespeare's sonnets, which had been much admired by Hallam, were an important model for Tennyson's poem. The effectiveness of the structure, which marks the passing of time and the progress through various stages of grief, cannot be exemplified by the brief selections included in this volume: read in full, *In Memoriam* is a long poem consisting of 131 separate but often closely linked lyrics with a prologue and an epilogue.

VII

1   *Dark house* 67 Wimpole Street, the London home of the Hallam family.

LIV–LVI

A linked series of poems expressing the challenge to orthodox Christian faith represented by nineteenth-century scientific thought: the New Testament's insistence on God's loving concern for every individual creature (LIV, stanzas 2 and 3) seems to be contradicted by the evidence of 'Nature' (LV, line 5) – that is, observation of the natural world and the universal struggle for existence. The evidence of geology (LVI, line 2) and of species once flourishing but now extinct (LVI, line 22: Tennyson's 'dragons' are presumably dinosaurs and other giant forms) suggests that humanity itself may be merely a stage in a mechanical process rather than the 'lord of creation' made in the image of God. Tennyson shows an awareness of current scientific ideas: Darwin's *Origin of Species* was not to appear until nine years after *In Memoriam*, but he was well acquainted with Sir Charles Lyell's work on geology and palaeontology, published in 1830–33, and other pioneering studies.

ODE ON THE DEATH OF THE DUKE OF WELLINGTON

Published 16 November 1852, two days before Wellington's funeral; he had died on 14 September. Wellington was the hero of the campaign against Napoleon and subsequently became a politician and prime minister. The crowd watching the funeral procession to St Paul's was estimated at one and a half million. Early in the following year Tennyson published a second edition, revised and expanded.

1   *Bury* in early editions this line begins 'Let us bury'; the first two words were dropped, with an increase in emphasis, in 1855.

42   *world-victor's victor* that is, the conqueror of Napoleon.

137   *Baltic, Nile* two of the victories, in 1801 and 1798 respectively, won by Nelson (the 'Mighty Seaman' of line 134).

155   *Briton* early editions have 'Saxon', the change being made in 1864.

THE CHARGE OF THE LIGHT BRIGADE

Written on 2 December 1854 and published one week later in *The Examiner*. The ill-fated charge in the Crimean campaign had taken place on 25 October and had been the subject of an editorial in *The Times* on 13 November in which had appeared the phrase 'some hideous blunder', adapted by Tennyson in line 12. Tennyson can be heard, faintly but fascinatingly, reading this poem on a wax cylinder recording made in about 1890.

17   *hundred* Tennyson's rhyming of this word with 'blundered' suggests that he gave it the Lincolnshire pronunciation 'hunderd'. Many who met Tennyson commented on his broad regional accent.

MAUD

Written 1854–5, published in 1855, and revised for later editions. The 'germ' of the poem, the lyric 'O that 'twere possible' (later incorporated in the poem and included in the extracts given in this volume), had been written in 1833–4 under the impact of Hallam's death. According to Tennyson's son he explained that ' "This poem of *Maud or the Madness* is a little *Hamlet*, the history of a morbid, poetic soul, under the blighting influence of a recklessly speculative age. . . . The peculiarity of this poem is that different phases of passion in one person take the place of different characters" ' – this latter remark explaining the poem's subtitle, 'A Monodrama'. *Maud* embodies many personal anxieties, including Tennyson's attitudes towards his father, his mother, his grandfather and his uncle Charles as well as his love for Rosa Baring and Emily Sellwood. (R. W. Rader's *Tennyson's 'Maud'* (1963) discusses these issues in detail.) Perhaps for this reason among others, Tennyson became addicted to reading and reciting the poem, and did so over a period of nearly forty years to almost anyone who would lend a sympathetic, or at least a willing, ear. The poem was widely attacked on its appearance, chiefly on the grounds of its morbidity and obscurity; the attitude to war expressed in the concluding section was also criticized by readers who forgot that in a dramatic monologue the protagonist's opinions are not necessarily those of the author. For some interesting examples of the contemporary response, see the collection edited by John Jump (cited in the Reading List).

Part I,I

33   *slurring* speaking disparagingly of.

34-46   the passage draws attention to contemporary social problems, including bad housing and the offences against morality that result from overcrowding (line 34).

37   *vitriol madness* 'Vitriol-throwing became a public menace during the 1840s, years of civil disobedience in Ireland and of social unrest in England' (Susan Shatto, whose edition of the poem very usefully annotates its numerous allusions). Vitriol is, strictly speaking, sulphuric acid, or, in popular usage, could refer to a wider range of chemical substances.

39–40   There were numerous cases of death through poisoning by adulterated foodstuffs, especially among the poorer classes.

41–2   *centre-bits* tools used by burglars; the reference is to the prevalence of crime that renders even the home unsafe.

43–4   The reference is to the widespread use of opium as a painkiller or sedative; it was freely available and was adulterated by unscrupulous druggists.

45   Cases of infanticide were motivated by the wish to claim a small sum from a 'burial club' providing insurance money intended to cover the cost of a funeral.

46   *Timour-Mammon* Timour is a form of the name Tamerlane, the medieval Tartar conqueror here synonymous with cruelty and indifference to human suffering; Mammon personifies the desire for wealth, as in the Gospels ('Ye cannot serve God and Mammon').

53–64   These stanzas were added in 1856.

76   *in myself* early editions read 'in my books', the revision being made in 1865.

IV

7   *eft* Tennyson explained the word as referring to 'One of the great old lizards of geology'.

7–12   Another passage that suggests the influence of Tennyson's